VAGABOND

CEILIDH MICHELLE

Vaga

bond

VENICE BEACH, SLAB CITY AND POINTS IN BETWEEN

Douglas & McIntyre

Douglas and McIntyre (2013) Ltd.
P.O. Box 219, Madeira Park, BC, VON 2H0
www.douglas-mcintyre.com

Edited by Caroline Skelton
Text design by Carleton Wilson
Cover photograph by Brad Donaldson, courtesy the author
Printed and bound in Canada
Printed on 100 per cent recycled paper

Supported by the Province of British Columbia

Douglas and McIntyre acknowledges the support of the Canada Council for the Arts, the Government of Canada, and the Province of British Columbia through the BC Arts Council.

LIBRARY AND ARCHIVES CANADA CATALOGUING IN PUBLICATION

Title: Vagabond : Venice Beach, Slab City and points in between / Ceilidh Michelle.
Names: Michelle, Ceilidh, 1987- author.
Identifiers: Canadiana (print) 20210231971 | Canadiana (ebook) 2021023203X | ISBN 9781771622981 (softcover) | ISBN 9781771622998 (EPUB)
Subjects: LCSH: Michelle, Ceilidh, 1987—Travel—California—Pacific Coast. | CSH: Authors, Canadian (English)—Travel—California—Pacific Coast. | CSH: Authors, Canadian (English)—21st century—Biography. | LCSH: Rogues and vagabonds—Travel—California—Pacific Coast. | LCSH: Rogues and vagabonds—Canada—Biography. | LCSH: Pacific Coast (Calif.)—Description and travel. | LCGFT: Autobiographies.
Classification: LCC PS8626.I275 Z46 2021 | DDC C818/.603—dc23

For Half-Peach

Contents

Author's Note

In December 2008 I went to California and lived there until the end of March 2009.

I wrote down everything that happened in a notebook. Most of the street names of the people included here are real, except for a few people I wanted to protect. Some of the situations have had their chaos smoothed, for clarity.

Slab City

"You hippies know what a serial killer is?" The man leaned against his orange car at the El Centro gas station, chewing on his lipless mouth. "You all wanna get to Slab City, it's an hour from here. Guess I can drive you, considering you ain't gonna get a ride this time of night."

The white gas station lights blazed the night away like a campfire keeping back wild animals. Half-Peach and I climbed into the car, Little Wing the chihuahua tucked under my arm.

"First landmark is Salvation Mountain. That's where the slabs start and that's as far as I go. I ain't gonna be navigating the crazy desert looking for some hobo's trailer. And that dog better not piss on the seat."

A white wood sign flew past the side of the car. *You're almost there.* Another sign, *Slab City Last Free Place on Earth,* went by with it.

The dark outside was a live thing, hot and quiet. Even the stars slept. We didn't say much. Half-Peach never did, and I was too worn out. It had taken us days to get to the desert. Before this we'd been in Ocean Beach. Before that, Los Angeles, Hollywood, Long Beach, Compton.

The man's car was thick with the fumes of a vanilla air freshener. He loudly played a country radio station. Half-Peach sat in the front seat and I sat in the back, piled in with the guitar and backpacks, the pocket of warmth that was Little Wing on my lap. I patted her sleek black fur and was glad for something to hold on to. The darkness pressed against the car windows like a bulk of velvet giants.

The entrance to Slab City began where the paved road ended. There was an old toll booth, long abandoned, and the vague, lumpy shape of Salvation Mountain, a sculptured maze of tunnels and murals, in the background. There were no lights and the night bore down, the air shot through with coyote song. Little Wing pricked up her ears to try and translate the language of her cousins.

When the orange car pulled away with a one-honk salute, we held our hands up in front of our faces and couldn't find them.

"I got a flashlight," Half-Peach said and tried to find it by running their hands over the junk in their bag. They had been to the slabs before. Half-Peach was an Aquarius and a Filipino introvert. They wore a straw hat on top of their black hair. They played banjo and came from the suburbs of Chicago. We'd known each other for one month. "Let's try and find the hot springs," they said, extracting their flashlight at last. Clicking it on and slicing a yellow beam through the blackness, they led the way across the desert scrub. They were light on their feet, using their tiptoes to walk. The flashlight's path shot a few feet ahead, turning the entire earth into a shadow.

"We'll set a tarp out here tonight and go over to the Karma Kitchen in the morning. Angel and Scooter will give us a place to sleep and some work," they told me as we stumbled along with our arms out for balance. Because Slab City was the last free place on earth, nothing could be gotten with cash. Not that we had any.

Half-Peach had been telling me about Slab City since I met them at a phone booth on the Venice Beach boardwalk. They'd told me it was possible to go into the neighbouring town of Niland and play guitar for gas, which could be brought back to Slab City and traded for cigarettes and food. There was also the Free Slab, an empty cement lot where people threw things they didn't want anymore. But that held little appeal for me. The more things I got, the more things I'd have to carry.

When we spotted the steam rising from the ground, we knew we had reached the hot springs. I tripped over muddy ruts following Half-Peach. We came to a clearing in the skeletal brush and I could see the risen moon glinting on opaque water.

"Talk loud so the coyotes don't come," Half-Peach warned. The dog-song could be heard from somewhere, wailing as they went. I held Little Wing tightly under my arm until we reached the lip of the pit, and then I put her down. She turned in circles and sat by the edge of the hot water.

"Hello kids. Water's perfect," a voice creaked up from the spring.

Half-Peach politely put the flashlight down, but I could just make out the old couple sitting in the middle of the pit, rubbing mud on each other's backs.

I peeled off my clothes and could smell how dirty they were as soon as they separated from me. I dropped my backpack to the ground. A plank ladder led down into the hot, thick water—it came up to my shoulders in an embrace of mud. On the bottom of the pit was a stretch of gritty carpet to keep feet from sinking in the slippery mire.

"Welcome to the slabs," the old woman said, intuiting we had arrived that night. Her voice was as old and kind as the moon.

"Watch out for that corner," the old man said. "That's where the pit goes down to the centre of the earth. Man last year had a heart attack when he got too close." We sat cross-legged on the dirty carpet squares in the hot, silty water and copied the old couple rubbing their faces with mud.

"It's good for you," she said, her shoulders shining in the moonlight.

Before the Beginning

The place I lived before I went away was a sprawling old apartment complex in Montreal, rising up from the sidewalk like a pile of trash. The owner was a hustling French-Canadian low-grade Mafioso who wore shoes with heels because he was barely five feet tall. He drove a black car through the narrow street, slow as a warning. I'd only glimpsed him in the hallways in passing, banging on the apartment doors to collect the rent, his long coat drawn around him.

Outside, the garbage was piled halfway up the side of the building: broken furniture, dangling clothes, mops and brooms all over the fire escape. Homeless people were always trying to get inside to sleep in the halls at night. There was a rumour of bedbugs, but I ignored it. I could only handle so much.

The hallways of the building were long and window-less, stale fluorescent lights flickering. A constant smell of piss emanated from the corners, and on the vestibule window a sun-faded sign eternally read, *Apartments for Rent.*

The concierge was a woman named Kitty: a stocky little wino with beige teeth, beady eyes and an acid tongue. If she caught you loitering in the hallway, she'd scream, "Pig! Pig!" until you popped your head back into your apartment. And then she'd totter down the hallway, picking at paint flecks with her fingernail.

I lived with a boy and things were often bad. He was unimportant in the span of things, but at the time I was in it and none of it felt as insignificant as it was. There were drugs. He was paranoid, often disappeared, and when he was gone, I went down the hallway to Thomas's place.

Thomas was an old man from Trinidad. He cooked Indian food every day; his whole place smelled of turmeric and lentil dal. He'd filled his living room with statues and paintings, all of them looking like they'd been left too long in the rain. The lights were never on, except for one old yellow lamp. His two cats, named after obscure Egyptian deities, could be heard yowling their cat song on the fire escape, just another element in the storm of chaos. Thomas used his bathtub as a place to hang his suits. The man was skinny as a tree branch, all brown and bone, and had a white moustache with orange nicotine stains. He said he spoke three languages—French, English and gibberish, because you couldn't understand a word he said when he spoke anyway.

Thomas had a telephone. I'd go over there to use it when the boy disappeared, to try and track him down. I'd knock and Thomas would open the door with a wordless nod. Then I'd come in, settle myself deep in the couch, and Thomas would put on a record, pour some brandy and roll a joint. I'd make my call, pet the cats. Thomas would stir whatever was on the stove. Sometimes he'd talk. Once he told me he'd been to other planets.

The days were destructively cold. Montreal winters had a way of tearing into your flesh. The boy sold drugs so we didn't have to work. Neither of us wanted me there but I stayed anyway, in the chilly, filthy apartment with the dirt-coloured floor and tweaked-out neighbours.

Outside, it was forty below and snowdrifts were thigh-high. People paced the floors like convicts and only went out if it was worth the frostbite.

Every time I came into the apartment, the boy would be sitting there sweating through the fever of some anxiety-induced mental fit. He said the people in the apartment below us were recording everything, stealing his songs and putting them on the radio. "You hear that?" he'd shout. "You hear that tapping noise? They're putting microphones up to the ceiling!" He'd stomp on the floor and shout down at them. Sometimes he'd grit his teeth and say, "I'm going down there. I'm going to tell them I know what they're fucking doing. I know what's going on. I'm going to leave a note on their door, man."

He came into the apartment one day, his eyes big, saying everyone out there was reading his thoughts, condemning him, getting into his head. He stopped wanting to have sex because he said it gave him a smell everyone could detect. He started washing his pants over and over again, sniffing them as soon as they came out of the dryer.

"You can still smell it," he'd say, throwing the pants back into the washer or sometimes throwing them straight into the garbage. One time he set his jeans on fire with his lighter.

He'd shower three times a day, scrubbing his skin, trying to wash it off, but it followed him, the smell of sin.

I smoked hundreds of cigarettes and became convinced I was having heart attacks. The boy and I had the kind of fights only young people do, where the world closes in and exists merely for the battle. I ripped up a bucket of yellow daisies and threw them across the white sheets of our bed. When I went out alone, he followed me down the street and hid behind parked cars to spy on me. There was a couch in the living room, and one of us slept on it every night. The world was running out of life.

I was cold and almost twenty-one. Thomas's phone could not call long-distance. One night I went down to the pay phone on the corner with a handful of quarters, doubled over in the razor blade wind, and called my sister in Vancouver. She said it was raining and the city was full of jobs. She had a couch. I could pay her back.

As a going away present, Thomas gave me a book with an orange cover. It was Paramahansa Yogananda's *Autobiography of a Yogi.*

The apartment was silent while my sister went out into the city to work. I stood by the window and stared at the ridges of blue teeth along the horizon, as if I were being devoured. I listened to the ticking of clocks, the drip of a water faucet. The streets of Vancouver were grey and strange, heavy with rain and loneliness.

The orange book was open on the floor like an illustration of a flying bird. I escaped into it every day. When Yogananda was a boy he hopped on a train, went off on a spiritual pilgrimage, with visions of success in his head. He travelled west. He prayed and his life sprung up around him, warm and sudden.

In the paperback book was a pamphlet advertising the ashrams he'd built in Nevada City. Vancouver was much closer to California than Montreal had been.

I left a handwritten note. My sister would understand. They should all understand. Why couldn't everyone walk out into the world with their belongings on their back and look for God? I had nothing. It felt like freedom.

Crossing Over

I was in Washington by the afternoon, on a Greyhound bus. I would arrive in the Sacramento terminal by nine the next morning, I thought, and would have the daylight to hitch to Nevada City.

But when it was my turn to be interrogated, it didn't go the way it was supposed to. The officer seemed seven feet tall and spoke slowly from a smug moustache. He called me little lady. "Little lady," he said, "There is no way I'm letting you into America." He sat me on one of the hallway benches like a child waiting to see the principal. The building was chilly and sterile. I had a soft case with an acoustic guitar, stuffed tight with clothes and my one book. The fluorescent atmosphere buzzed and hummed with electricity, smelled of plastic-wrapped sandwiches and glass cleaner, and beneath those smells, a whiff of the road, tar melting in the sun.

I'd given them the phone number of my contact, a friend-of-a-friend I'd never met and never would. I only knew he lived in Echo Park and people called him Johnny

Longhair. This wasn't enough. The officer wanted bank statements, proof of addresses, date of return.

But there was no way back. I sat marooned in concrete and industrial lights. The thin line of fellow Greyhound passengers shuffled past, looking guiltily at their feet. If they saw me, they might become me.

"Next bus back to Vancouver is in three hours. You'll be on it," the officer said. He hovered over me for a moment, waiting for me to realize the weight of his absolute power. Then he went on into his glass-walled cubicle, sat at his desk and dipped his moustache in a mug of coffee. Smiling.

Around me, scattered groups of travellers came blinking into the prison-styled building, coming and going, offering up their papers and being released back to their vehicles, free to go wherever they were going. I watched the light cross the tiled floor, fade. I prayed, *This was not how this was supposed to go.* I clutched my book. I waited for something else to happen.

There were no clocks on the wall, but my body felt several hours had gone by when the moustached officer finally stood and stretched. He strolled past me, moving freely through the doors to the parking lot, climbed into his car and drove off through the gates of the barbed-wire fence.

He was efficiently replaced by another officer, this one bright-eyed and barely grown. He came dancing into the customs office, sat in the glass cubicle and beckoned with a finger.

"You miss your bus?" He gestured me into a plastic chair.

"I was trying to get to California." I called him sir because I figured he'd appreciate it.

"What for?" He had typed my name into the computer. He could probably see I'd been blacklisted or barricaded or blocked.

I held up *Autobiography of a Yogi*. "I didn't have enough money in my bank account. But I'm going to an ashram. I read this book."

The guard leaned forward conspiratorially, put his elbows up on the desk as if he were going to share a piece of gossip. His eyes were wide and pure and blue. I could count the hairs of his first moustache crawling along his lip. "Look. The next bus for California comes in four hours. I'm going to put you on it. You're going to go for your little pilgrimage and you're going to come right back. Capisce?"

"Capisce."

I had to sleep overnight in the Seattle bus station on a bench cold as an ice sculpture. People lurked around the terminal, somnolent thugs in a seedy dream. The security guard asked me to come sit beside his booth. I used my bag as a pillow. I half-dreamed a neon Jacob's Ladder falling from the fluorescent lights and taking me up.

Because of the delay at customs, I arrived in Sacramento at three in the morning. The bus station felt like a fallout shelter, cinder-block walls scrawled with phone numbers, cocks, eyeballs, illegible promises. The immortalizations of long-gone highway drifters: *Sandra wuz Here*. Beneath dim lights moved throngs of men: big men, old men, angry men, tired men. They hustled their way from the bus to the terminal and back again, putting their razors and chains and suitcases into plastic bins for examination. The terminal employees called directions and instructions in a monotone. I couldn't sleep on the benches. I was one situation away from something stupid and dangerous.

When a neon-vested employee announced a connection to Los Angeles, the nebulous ashram of Nevada City dissolved in the buzzing light. I got back on the bus.

Somewhere outside Sacramento, the bus stopped at a town that was nothing more than a strip of buildings in the night. A round blond girl got on and sat beside me. She told me her name was Caroline.

"I'm a missionary," she said. "I was just in Africa teaching children about the Lord."

"I'm going to Los Angeles," I said and showed her my book.

The girl smiled politely.

"I was supposed to go to his ashram, but he has temples in Los Angeles, too. I guess that's where I'm going now."

"The Lord works in mysterious ways," the girl said. She fell asleep in five minutes.

I watched the land rippling past the windows. I held my book. I didn't sleep.

Hollywood spangled in stars and palm fronds. The names of actors immortalized in rain-splashed sidewalks. I climbed down from an inner-city bus and went into a shop burning incense and candles. Krishna hung from silver necklaces in the window. Shiva with his dancing arms dangled from earrings.

I asked the woman enshrined behind the cash register if she knew where I could find the temples of Paramahansa Yogananda. She shrugged. "I'm Hindu," she said. "I worship Krishna."

The city buses were orange and lurid as neon fruit. I stood on the sidewalk and picked one that said *Venice Beach*.

"You love Jesus?" the bus driver screamed in my face, his teeth white and bright as the letters on the hill. There was a rainbow across the windshield as he handled the heavy bus through the glittering streets. "Jesus don't give a shit what you done," he cried, putting his arm out to keep the passengers from falling against his seat. The street hissed wetly as it lay flat beneath the tires. "Jesus love you anyway. He ain't gonna roast you. That's why he died. People can't get the simple stuff. They gotta make it all complicated. Nobody goin to hell. They already there."

People kept pushing onto the bus, damp and smelling of old rubber. And this bus driver grinning and shouting, "Jesus loves you! You love Jesus?" People nodded back, jangling the change in their pockets, saying, "Sure, why not?"

The bus made it to the beach. I walked along the cold sand and stuck my fingers in the foam of the sea.

I had enough money for two nights at a hostel. The building looked like a forgotten sandcastle, a Moulin Rouge, Atlantis with painted pillars peeling in the salt air of the night. *Venice* was strung in white letters through the sky, fairy lights replacing the stars that had vanished under the lid of constant smog. The boulevard was a travelling circus caught in a frame of sharp winter light.

I slept in a bunk bed in a room with six strangers who came and went, anonymous through the hours.

In the book, it said Paramahansa Yogananda had his International Headquarters up in Mount Washington, the hills north of the city. I took the bus from Venice Beach. The drive took almost three hours, past industrial-looking palm trees, stretched-out box stores, boulevards of sparkling cars. Mar Vista, Culver City, Arlington Heights. I got off near Chinatown and walked the last hour in a drizzling rain over the Los Angeles River, up wide white roads that wound around the hills. I could see out over the valleys of the city, the highways and neighbourhoods sprawling toward the horizon line.

The incline was steep, my shins burning as I bent over to breathe. A lone dog barked from somewhere in a sideways lawn. Low-slung stucco houses were stacked into the hillside, tucked back beneath pepper trees, pickup trucks parked in driveways winding into private lives hidden behind slatted fences. They didn't even know I was there, hiking past them to the top of the mountain to find a temple I'd only read about.

The hilltop road wound down into a dip between trees whose hands met above my head, creating a green tunnel. I walked across the wet road and through the gate of a towering wrought iron fence. As soon as I entered the grounds, a silence came down as if a pair of soft hands went over my ears. The gravel path took me to the headquarters, a clean, white, square building standing tall among the lushness.

The doors were open. I went up the stairs, holding my book like a passport. The carpets were deep and red and there was a desk in the entrance, like a hotel. The air was smoky with incense. To the right of me was a massive portrait of the guru. A shorn nun in yellow robes greeted me in a German accent. She asked me where I had come from to make the visit. I said Canada. I told her I hiked the mountain.

"You could have called," she said. "We send a car down for visitors." She was smiling.

"Oh." I stood there stupidly. I thought I would show up and then I would know what to do with myself, that something would feel satisfied or be made clear. But that hadn't happened. The nun began to turn away and I stood in the lobby, my toes sinking into the deep carpet, breathing the smell of nag champa. Renunciants came and went through the door, their bodies loose and peaceful. Some of them went up staircases into the depths of the building. I wanted someone to say they'd been waiting for me. But I was scruffy and anonymous, some unremarkable youth without money to pay for a yoga program, the bad habits of a runaway.

I could see I was going to lose the nun, so I blurted, "What do I have to do to stay here? How do I become a renunciant?" I gestured at her ochre robe. I wanted her to cut off all my hair and take me to a room where all the noise would fall away.

"How old are you?" she asked me.

"Twenty-one."

"Why'd you come all this way? What did you come here for?"

"I want to be a monk. I mean a nun," I said. That was it. And I had no place to go. But I didn't tell her that part.

"Well." She indicated the front desk, the informational pamphlets. "We don't use ascetic life as a shelter. We are always in the world. But I saw enough that I was satisfied when I came. Do you think you've seen enough?" She'd already made up her mind about me. I was dissatisfied. "There is the guide." The nun jutted her chin toward a bored-looking old man near the door and then strolled slowly away. What would they do, the bored old man and the front desk person, the yellow nun, if I bolted upstairs into the quiet folds of the building?

The old man made his way over. "Come, let me show you the leader's library," he said in the monotone of someone who had guided a thousand obnoxious tourists. I was just another one of those. He herded me into a room off the side of the lobby.

Again, the plush odour of incense. A dark wooden desk and, on the shelf behind it, a few bound books. The tall windows looked out into the trees. The guru's private library. It was so quiet here I could hear the breath come up inside me. My fingers on my paperback book.

The guide said, "They always want to know what the guru was reading," pointing at the shelf of books. "They should be more interested in the book *he* wrote."

I held up my copy. But the man only nodded, made a noncommittal noise of approval. Would he pass this along to the German nun?

I followed him back out into the golden foyer. "Here now is the meditation hall," he said, ushering me back through the lobby to the other side. A set of double doors opened into darkness. He extended a hand like a fat starfish. "Silence please." I hadn't spoken.

A monolithic painting of Paramahansa Yogananda hung at the front of the room. At the foot of it stuttered a hundred candles, messy smoking bouquets of incense sticks. It looked like the guru was sitting on a cloud of smoke. Devotees huddled on the carpet, hunched over with their faces in their laps, rocking, running beads through their fingers. I stood in the doorway, choking on incense fumes. Was I expected to sit and meditate with the strangers?

The guide stared at me. After we stood there for several strained minutes, he hissed, "You must go in and meditate or go out to the grounds. You cannot stand here halfway."

In the shadows a few people glanced over at me. I'd distracted them with my restlessness. The guide waded into the shadows. He found a pillow and sat.

No one noticed as I slipped from the temple, back out into the jungle of the misty grounds. Tucked into the side of the path was a little wooden bench and I sat on that for a while. It began to rain but I was dry beneath the branches.

The sound of the rain infiltrated the silence with its pattering sounds, and as the afternoon climbed on, I noticed a few wandering tourists. I sat there waiting. Nothing happened. I looked up at the blank windows of the towering headquarters, but they were empty. When the rain tapered off, I stood and stretched my legs and walked back down the mountain.

Beginning

The early December air was murky with humidity. I was at a café on Abbot Kinney called Abbot's Habit, sitting on one of the wooden blocks that served as chairs, smoking cigarettes and watching. People milled around on the sidewalk, some of them already positioned under the green awning, anticipating the coming rain.

I'd been in Los Angeles for a week, staying in a camper with a middle-aged man named Tad whom I'd met on the boardwalk. I slept in a bunk above the driver's seat and he slept on a fold-out table below. But I couldn't go back there anymore.

The night before, protected by darkness, he told me about his niece, how she was five years old but had given him a hard-on when he'd touched her ass.

I woke at dawn, but Tad had already left for the day. I grabbed my things and left a note on his windshield saying I was moving on. I sat cross-legged on the cold sidewalk with my acoustic guitar, put my hat down in front of me and played songs for some breakfast.

Abbot Kinney was awash with yoga teachers and surfers and computer designers, museum curators, gallery owners, celebrities, executive producers. Mixing among them were poverty-ruined wanderers, crust punks from the Midwest who had come for the sun, peddling crystal jewellery, playing banjos or blatantly begging for change. Across the street the steel-and-glass yoga gym promised *No granola! No chanting! No Sanskrit!* on its front window. The locals strolled up and down Abbot Kinney with their longboards and hemp pants, distressed leather bags, yoga mats, salted hair. They could grab a latte and head back to their minimalistic condominiums. They could get in their cars and drive out of the sprawl to the canyons. The absolute definition of money was happiness, I thought, and only a fool would deny this truth.

As I sat there, Tad came wandering up, dropping a five-dollar bill into my hat.

"Got your goodbye note. You don't want to continue on to Mexico with me?" He sheepishly rubbed his sunburned face, a faded baseball cap pushed back on his head. When he'd found me alone on the boardwalk that first night and we'd got to talking, we found out we were both from Vancouver. How bad could a Canadian man be? He said I could think of him as a father, but I just needed a place to sleep. Now I did again.

I couldn't imagine being in Mexico City with Tad and his camper van. I looked up at him from where I sat on the sidewalk, the winter light making me squint. "I think this is as far as I'm going," I told him.

All I knew of Neptune, Kasey and Kriel was what I'd seen and heard in the last five minutes at Abbot's Habit. Neptune had driven to Venice Beach from Texas to meet his half-brother Kasey for the very first time. Kasey came all the way from Colombia. Kriel was big and pink, gold hair down to her waist. She sat cross-legged like a Buddha, her eyes half-closed.

"We're gonna make a movie," Neptune said. "Have its story go from Colombia to Los Angeles. From Texas to right here." He patted the top of the table with his dark brown hand. "It'll trace the path of synchronicity and spirituality. Mojave Desert. Joshua Tree." He made a figure eight in the air with his fingertip. The inside of his palm pink as a shell. "I did time in county and when you're inside it makes your mind want to do something that'll make you more of a person." He tugged on the springy tips of his hair.

Kasey's sombre expression was a weird contrast to his brown baby face and sweetheart mouth. But I think he was trying to be the logical one. "What'd the producer say?"

I noticed the blond woman taking minutes of their meeting in a notebook, the pages of which were bright purple.

"Said he works with Street People. I dunno what makes somebody a Street Person, but if it involves us getting our project funded, so be it." Neptune tilted back his head to drink the last grains of his coffee.

People talked that way in Venice Beach, the people in patched denim and flower patterns, dreadlocks and train maps, banjos and harmonicas. Urban hillbillies roaming the highways and chasing the sun, pawing through dumpsters and sleeping outside. Making crystal jewellery and selling it on the boardwalk, sitting on a paisley scarf. Prophets of their own freedom theories. Seers without futures lying on the sand, they dismissed practicality as faithlessness. Raving about their salvation projects, talking of the towns they'd left behind, where there was easy food and less danger but no liberty. I guess I was one of these people too, just by virtue of hanging around.

"When's he coming?" The woman spoke low and calm. She brushed hair from her eyes and looked over at me, as if she knew I'd been watching. I busied myself lighting another cigarette.

"He said noon." Neptune stared at the sky as if trying to tell the time.

"It's noon now," Kasey said, checking his watch.

Their producer came ambling up the sidewalk then, grey hair tucked neatly under a baseball cap. He carried a coffee cup from somewhere else. "Gang's all here?" he said by way of greeting.

"We're just waiting for one more." The woman shoved over on the block so there was room for me. I went as automatically as walking through a dream. She pulled me into her bready side. "Wanna be in our movie?"

The rooted comfort of being taken in by a family, of not being alone in the night, was warm as wine. I said, "Sure, I'll be in your movie."

The producer grabbed a wooden block, his grin bemused and lopsided as he looked us over. "Let's start, shall we? Tell me about this project of yours."

"It's gonna be a documentary," Neptune began, "about us. My brother and me. We met through serendipity."

"Serendipity? How's that?" The producer pushed up his glasses. He wanted facts, not hallucinations. People in Los Angeles seemed wary of idealism—it never ended well.

"We have the same mother," Neptune said, "but she died last year. That's when I found out I had a brother."

"Ah. Okay. Because the angle I'm seeing here," and the producer framed a shot of the street with his fingers, "is a piece on travellers, the youth that keep making these hitchhiking pilgrimages to Los Angeles, to Venice Beach. Through the framework of you folks. I mean, you for example." He turned to the blond woman who was spread out like watercolours. "Where'd you come from?"

"I'm from California."

"Oh." The producer turned to me. "Okay, you. You don't look like you're from Los Angeles."

"I'm from Canada."

The blond woman and the boys turned to me with interest. Neptune said, "Really? I never met one of you before." He shook my hand. "I'm Neptune, this is my new brother, Kasey. And that's Kriel," he nodded over at her. Kriel jostled me against her with affection.

"Wait, wait, wait," the producer interjected. "I thought you said you were *waiting* for her ... and then she came and sat down. You don't even know each other?" He took off his glasses, wiping frantically at the lenses with his T-shirt.

"This is the movie, man! This right here. You should be filming this!" Neptune banged his hand on the table.

"I'm a producer," the producer said.

"What my brother means," Kasey interjected, "is that this film is about connections young people make when they're looking for somewhere to go. The days are spontaneous and uncertain. Bonds are immediate and profound. The film is about how we survive, how we navigate a racist, capitalistic system that has made outsiders of us, forcing us to live on the fringes of society. The cameras have to follow us everywhere."

The producer shrugged. "Sounds fun. Anyway, all the money is coming from West Hollywood. We have an organization that allocates funds for ... social justice projects. I know they wanna work with ... minority groups mostly. So you two are good to go." He nodded at Neptune and Kasey.

Kriel began to braid my hair. Her hands were so soothing that I closed my eyes. The producer's staccato details,
the traffic from Venice Boulevard, the chatter of the café
patrons, washed over me like the sunlight along the street.

After the producer got into his silver car and motored
back up into the hills, Neptune asked me if I was hungry,
which I always was. "Come on, we know a place." I followed Kasey, Kriel and Neptune from the café through the
side streets of Venice Beach—they were as sure about the
route as if they had grown up in the neighbourhood.

The whole area felt like a grotto. Low white bunga-
lows set back in shaggy yards shielded by the hands of
tropical leaves, sunlight dappling the wide streets. Neptune and his brother pointed out their black truck along
the way. They'd made the back into a bed and had been
sleeping in it. I peeked in its window as we walked past.
Translucent scarves hung down like those of an opium
den. "We can fit ten kids in there," Neptune bragged.

We wound up at the Church of Saint Mark, red roof
tiles, an arching door. The sun went away again, and it
began to rain lightly. Neptune led us through the parking
lot. He seemed to know the deacon.

"Hi kids, good timing. We have lunch on the go," the
deacon called from the open door, shepherding us inside the
church's social hall. The room had concrete floors and fluorescent lights, a folding table with food set out, coffee, tea. It
was as if they had prepared all this for us. "Sit, sit," he said.

There were the sounds of women in the kitchen like distant birds. The deacon came in and out with Styrofoam plates heaped with warm heavy things, pasta, bread, potatoes. The plastic chair was cold under my legs.

Neptune and Kasey sat on either side of me, Kriel across the table. We smiled at each other as if this right here had been our plan all along.

That night I slept in the truck, parked under the trees. Neptune and Kasey had layered the bed with quilts and sleeping bags. Climbing inside was like being buried. The back of the truck was crowded with kids they brought in from the beach.

There was a girl named Carolina with hair down to her ass. The beauty of her face was disarming—it seemed dangerous in a place like this. She said she had run away from home after her mother married a terrible man. Her eyes glazed over as she talked. Kriel whispered that the girl was heavily medicated. During the day Carolina ran around the beach, spaced out, easily seduced, often in trouble.

There was Frederick, too. He was a rail-thin, flamboyantly queer boy with a long red beard. He'd come from Eastern Europe to be an American beatnik, but so far, he'd only gotten beat up on the streets behind the beach. At night, Frederick read his poetry aloud in the truck while we passed around a bottle of Two Buck Chuck, red wine from Trader Joe's.

And Juan. He had been brought from Mexico when he was little. Both his parents had been immediately deported. Juan disappeared, slipping between the cracks of the disorganized city. He was mute. During the days, no one knew where he went or what he did, but Neptune and Kasey found him waiting by their truck every night, holding a bottle of wine in exchange for shelter.

Kriel was somewhere in her late twenties. She made sure everyone was fed. She communicated for Juan. She protected Frederick. She kept an eye on Carolina. And now she did those things for me. Kriel emanated warmth and just as I had been drawn to a place with no winter, I was attracted to her for the same lack of coldness.

Sometimes kids came to the truck at night to peek their heads in, passing a joint through the window, and Neptune would hand them out a bottle of wine. They congregated around the truck in the twilight streets of Venice Beach to hear about Neptune's movie as if it were a ticket to glory for all of them.

"It's the only reason I'm here, it's the only reason I'm alive," he lectured.

That first night in the truck, I didn't sleep. I rolled around under the blankets with the litter of warm bodies pressed against my back. Neptune, lying beside me, opened his eyes and kissed me on the mouth, and it seemed like I was dreaming because then we fell asleep.

41

In the mornings, Neptune held court from his table at Abbot's Habit. The producer had given him a cellphone with the promise he'd call. While Neptune and Kasey discussed the cost of their ideas, waiting anxiously for the phone call, Kriel and I walked arm in arm along the boardwalk. I told her about Paramahansa Yogananda, and Kriel said, "Of course that's why you're here," as if it were the most natural thing in the world, me following a guru to the coast, Neptune following his post-prison dreams to find his lost brother, Kriel wandering down through the country for no reason at all. It didn't seem like I was on a pilgrimage anymore. I was no longer searching.

We'd meet up later in front of Big Daddy's, the bright blue pizza shack, and go out onto the sand, sitting there until the sun went down. The grasping, the hustling, quieted down when we were together. We'd found a little family in each other. We would sit on the beach every night and watch Pacific Ocean sunsets and write screen-plays and someday have a real house. Of course that's what would happen because it was what we wanted.

The homeless youth in Venice Beach were constantly looking for places to sit without getting harassed by cops, without business owners telling them they were in the way. Behind Abbot's Habit, on California and Electric Avenues, was the Youth and Family Center with a wide, sloping yard. The yard was a fine place to congregate. Besides the boardwalk, which could get overstimulating at best and dangerous at worst, there weren't many places to go without money. Kids often gathered at the centre with their dogs, sitting in circles, smoking, wire-wrapping crystals to sell on the beach.

One afternoon, Neptune, Kasey and I climbed into the back of the truck to take an afternoon nap. The winter sun was soft-edged, and we lay there talking.

"We can do anything in America," Neptune told me. Kasey lay on the other side. We stared up at the ridged truck roof as if we were watching the clouds.

Kasey said, "We can drive as far as the land goes."

They had a joint going back and forth, and the truck filled up with pearly smoke. "The whole world is doing what we're doing, wandering around and searching," said Neptune. "Only difference between us and them is we *know* we're searchers." Neptune exhaled smoke, where it hung like the Milky Way. "What do you think about having sex with both of us at the same time? Is it weird because we're brothers?"

I pinched the joint between my fingers. "I'm not sure if that's the weird part."

When we got out of the truck, the kids sitting in the yard made jokes about what they thought we'd been doing, but we hadn't done anything yet.

Neptune was in the Trader Joe's getting more Two Buck Chuck, and Kriel was with him. Kasey and I stood around in the parking lot.

"We should be using every available second to sharpen our minds. Our minds are weapons. We have to oil them, clean them, use them," Kasey said.

I thought guiltily of my orange book, shoved in my guitar case. I did not meditate, but every day I was in my head, walking through my own prayer. I didn't need to sit alone to be here now.

"Let's play telepathy." Kasey licked his lips and closed his eyes. "Get a place in your mind. I'm gonna try and see it."

I closed my eyes and the sounds and smells of Los Angeles came in: the salted air, the traffic jams, birdsong and crashing surf, the shush of wind through the leaves, musicians calling to each other in the parking lot, the dapples of light on the insides of my eyelids.

The California air was underpinned with the whispers of cult leaders, the rush of car tires on the highway, dollar bills rustling into hands, the scream of electric guitar, motorcycles tearing through the canyons, the rattle of palm fronds, the mellow morning breeze on my face.

"Got it," I said and pictured Vancouver, quiet and white and expensive, its cold water, the Squamish, the Musqueam.

Kasey's eyelids fluttered. I could see his hands moving inside his jean pockets. His toes curling in his shoes. "I see water," he said. "Not tropical. Grey. And blue and ... forget it, I got distracted."

"You two ready to go?" Neptune called across the parking lot, holding a bottle of wine in the air.

That night, Neptune pulled the truck's curtains closed and pressed a cardboard sign into the window saying, *Go Away.*

Cold raindrops of condensation dripped from the roof of the truck onto my skin. I was the first one to wake up. The blankets pushed down to the bottom of the mattress, empty wine bottles, condom wrappers. Kriel winked at me and then went back to sleep, Neptune's arm slung across her naked stomach.

When Neptune said he wanted to do research, I suggested we go to the library. He could take us in his truck to the Santa Monica branch, away from the closeness of Venice Beach. The Santa Monica Public Library was a white geometric edifice surrounded by palm trees, like something from a comic book. Neptune drove and Kriel sat beside him in the front. Kasey and I lay on the bed in the back, and from the mattress, I watched the city fly past overhead, the tops of anonymous buildings, the speck of a seagull, the tips of palm trees.

At the library, Kriel and Neptune pulled out books

on Machu Picchu, Atlantis, the psychedelic adventures of Carlos Castaneda, all the books we felt were required for this project, and then sat at a library table surrounded by volumes. Neptune had a piece of paper and a red crayon. "Cartography," he announced. "I'm going to make us a treasure map. And when we come to X Marks the Spot, we'll be enlightened, and everything will be made right."

Kasey kicked my foot under the table. He got up and disappeared between the shelves. After a few minutes, I stood and stretched. Kriel and Neptune didn't notice.

Kasey ducked behind a rack of pulp fiction. I went the other way through the room, could see him disappearing and reappearing as he wove around the books.

He went through the glass front doors. I looked behind me and followed him out. When we reached the truck, he pushed me inside onto the mattress.

"Why did you leave?" Kriel asked me.

"We're supposed to stick together, all of us," said Neptune. But his eyes were dark and already looking away.

The next night, Neptune drove us to Trader Joe's to get wine. He was silent behind the wheel. Kriel sat beside him. Kasey and I were in the back but this time under the blankets. I know they heard him spit out the condom wrapper he tore with his teeth.

When we got to the store, Neptune slammed on the brakes, and he and Kriel went in without us. When they came back, we were outside smoking cigarettes under the street lights, counting the moths that flew against the beam.

Kasey and Neptune decided to head to Corral Canyon on an overnight trip, just the two of them. "We need to regroup," Neptune told us.

They left early in the morning. Kriel and I saw them off from Abbot's Habit. Neptune's face was grim and determined, his hair the last thing visible through the windshield as they drove away.

Venice Beach had been a geode, an ugly rock only revealing its amethysts when broken open. But without the four of us together, Venice Beach took the shape of whatever was happening, street-tough and toxic, occult-heavy, gentrified and violent, lonely and inaccessible.

Without Neptune, there was no movie, no plan, no map.

After the black truck disappeared, Kriel said, "Now that it's just us, we should have a day of feminine energy. A spa day."

"A spa?" I said. I had never been to a spa. But I knew that out here we made our own versions of luxury.

At Ocean Park Community Center in Santa Monica, we could get a hot shower and a warm meal. Kriel and I walked there, following the beach from Venice to the sand of Santa Monica. While we walked, Kriel told me she'd been in Quartzsite, Arizona, before Los Angeles. Many of the travellers who made jewellery went back and forth from Quartzsite to Venice Beach. There were gem trade shows and full moon parties. Those were the kinds of things Kriel enjoyed.

"Is that how you met Neptune and his brother?" I asked, shading my face against the jagged sun. The sand was hot and shifted beneath my feet. Seagulls making broken cries above us as we went.

"In Arizona? No, we met here on the beach. I did a tarot reading for Neptune. The cards said we're twin flames."

The cards never lied. That's something people said on the boardwalk. I liked to hear people talk about things they believed in. I believed none of it, but I wanted to believe all of it.

"I'd marry him if he wasn't already," Kriel sighed, waving to someone she knew as we walked: one of the drug dealers with a coveted apartment on the boardwalk. His name was Noah. Pants belted below his ass, red bandana tied around his ears. He waved solemnly back at her, staring us down until we'd passed.

"Neptune's married?"

"And has a baby girl. They're back in Texas. Kasey keeps trying to convince him to go home and take responsibility, but Neptune ..." she grinned, flipping the gold scarves of her hair over her shoulder and hitching up her long skirt. "He's on a mission."

"What do you think he should do?"

Kriel shrugged. "I only know what *I* wanna do. I wanna have babies. But the doctor said I'm barren."

OPCC had the air of a government building: cinder-block walls, tiled floors, fluorescent lights. But it was clean, and people lined up politely around the outer wall, waiting for bagged lunches and taking plastic numbered cards for a shower.

When Kriel and I got our turn, someone handed us rubber flip-flops and tiny hotel shampoos. I stood under the hot water for a long time. The women in the steaming shower room wandered around wet and naked, hair dripping onto their shoulders. They chatted and laughed, their voices echoing, white plastic shower curtains rattling.

Kriel had inverted nipples. She stood in front of the mirror, staring at her reflection and running her fingers through her wet hair. When I came over, she looked into the reflection of my eyes. "Neptune and I have been in love for many lives," she said. "That's how I know something is wrong. He's gone too far out."

If Kriel thought he was getting too far out, he was probably long gone.

I didn't know what to say. "He'll be okay and you'll be okay and I'll be okay," I managed. But inside my head, there were no star signs or destined paths, no cosmic convictions other than my own survival.

That night Kriel and I went to sleep on the beach. The boardwalk was silent and awash in fog. The sunglasses huts and sandwich boards for cannabis clinics were all closed and shuttered in the dark. The fog accumulated quickly around us, opaque as smoke.

Suddenly we were the only two people on the boardwalk. The fog was static as if we had entered a white room. We couldn't see five feet ahead or behind us. There wasn't a sound. I wrapped my arms around myself. There was an awful coldness but no wind.

Kriel touched my arm and we stood perfectly still. I held my breath, my pulse pounding through me. "Something terrible is going to happen," she whispered.

A couple days later, the black truck came rolling down Market Street and pulled up beside Big Daddy's. Kriel and I had been drifting around with a local girl named Dahlia, a redhead from South Central wearing what looked like a lot of black, greasy rags. Dahlia taught us to wrap crystals in fine copper wire and make pendants. We helped her put them together, pinching the pliant wire into spirals with needle-nose pliers, and when she sold them to tourists, we got a cut.

Kriel and I were sitting on a blanket and sharing a sandwich when the black truck parked across the street. Only Kasey got out. He'd been driving. We could see Neptune hugging his knees in the front seat, staring out the side window as if the truck were still driving and he was watching the road.

Kasey crouched next to us. There were purple bags under his eyes. The other girls looked at him with distrust. They knew him as the brother of the cult leader. Or the one who held orgies in the back of his truck. The South American hustler. But I had listened as he told me about nursing his sick mother until her death. His departure from South America, following some vague dream to keep his family together. If he was a hustler then so was I.

"How was the trip?" Kriel asked, tentatively rubbing his hair.

"Fucked," said Kasey. "He didn't sleep. He ran out into the desert at night. He kept taking this root or vine or something. He said he had visions but wouldn't tell me what they were. He went wild. Maybe it was the heat. We wandered during the day out in the bush and at one point, I lost sight of him and could hear him screaming, just screaming ..." Kasey pressed on his eyes, sucked in his breath slowly. "I gotta get him back to Texas."

I could feel the white fog pounding.

That afternoon Kasey packed up the truck. Neptune hadn't moved from the front seat, his eyes wide and bulging, almost vibrating. He continued to hug his knees, rocking back and forth like he was on the ocean.

A few of us stood around in the sun, Juan, Carolina, Frederick, helping Kasey make up the bed in the back. As Kasey hopped behind the wheel, Kriel grabbed his arm.

"He needs me." And she nodded at Neptune, lost to the world around him. She climbed into the truck and wrapped him in her arms. He didn't even notice.

"If you're coming, come," Kasey told her. And then he looked at me, seeing what I would do.

But how could I leave Venice Beach? I couldn't be a part of someone else's homecoming. I didn't know anything about Texas. Under the sun punching its way through pyrite clouds, I didn't need to tell them yes or no. They knew I wasn't coming.

The black truck pulled off into traffic, and then Juan and Carolina and Frederick slowly and separately wandered away. The truck was all we had in common.

Little Wing

I wanted a dog. Many travellers on the boardwalk had dogs—they said the night seemed safer with a constant friend. I wanted another pair of eyes to watch the world with, making sure I didn't get caught in its craziness. I saw the way travellers went around with their dog friends, feeding them food they scored, walking together like witches with familiars, united in the long, unpredictable days. People knew not to mess with dogs, or if they did, it sent a specific message: they were going after your heart.

Along the morning side streets, seagulls sang their start-of-day songs. The sky pale blue and fresh before the car fumes reached it. I could have been anyone in the neighbourhood, running my errands and enjoying the sun.

Abraham owned a trailer in the parking lot at the end of the boardwalk; he'd painted it with a trillion pixelated dots, a patchy psychedelic sea. His wife had a smaller version of his trailer, painted the same and parked behind.

Every morning in the pink dawn he hauled his paintings onto the boardwalk, still wet and glistening, reeking of turpentine. He leaned them against the rock wall or put them flat on the ground. Abraham painted on pocked cupboard doors and long, frayed pieces of canvas, street signs, shreds of bald rubber tire and fishnetted driftwood, his brown, gnarled hands covered in colours, his dreadlocks matted with age and crusted with salt and sand. He even had paint on his toenails. His bare feet skimmed the sidewalk.

Along with the daily paintings, Abraham brought out big clear garbage bags full of bread, old donuts, hardened bagels. The bread was for anyone—he offered it to people and threw it to the gulls. I think he knew someone from a restaurant nearby, and they gave it to him at the end of the day. Abraham knew everyone on the boardwalk: film crews and celebrities, drug dealers and gang members, local mothers. His accent sounded as if it had come across the ocean, from an island far away, but he was one of the most local locals on the Venice Beach boardwalk.

His dog had just had a litter of puppies and so I went to see him.

By the time I got there Abraham had been out in front of his trailer for hours, new paintings dripping into the grass, his plastic bag of old bread already laid out.

54

When he saw me coming, he held up his pink-palmed hand in salute. He only spoke when necessary. I told him I wanted one of his puppies and he asked, "What you got?" Just because we boardwalk-dwellers had no money didn't mean anything was free.

Abraham's wife stood in the shade of the trailer with her back to us, watching the ocean like she was waiting for someone. She spoke less than her husband and still managed to be an irreplaceable fixture on the boardwalk.

The dogs ran circles in the grass. Abraham watched them proudly, nodding at passersby and directing them with his jutted chin to look at the dogs. The mother of the litter was a spaniel, as perfect as a china figurine. Smiling at the sun, her coat flowing white with brown polka dots. The father was a muscly black Chihuahua with brown markings. He tore about the parking lot like an overzealous demon, mad eyes bulging.

What strange splice these dogs would produce I did not know, but Abraham went into the trailer and came back out with his arms full of fat, wiggling puppies. Two boys, pure white, had inherited their mother's face and their father's Chihuahua body. Abraham deposited them in the grass, where they toppled over and lay panting in the sunshine.

Abraham looked at me and then said, "I'll be right back. I know what it is now." He vanished back inside his trailer and came out with the last puppy, the litter's runt, the sister. Her black fur gleamed in the sharp early morning sun of Venice Beach, her brown eye-markings like little wings. Abraham put her down on the boardwalk and her spindly legs shook before giving out. I picked her up and tucked her under my chin, walking around with her like the boardwalk was my own maternity ward.

For the next three weeks, I came every morning and stood with Abraham as he put out his bread and paintings. His wife watching the ocean, shielding her eyes from the sun and waiting for whatever it was she was waiting for.

When the little pup could walk, she recognized me coming and ran shakily across the grass, licking my hand with her pink tongue. She wasn't a big dog and some of the travellers scorned me for that, but her company was enough.

By the time she was ready to go with me, I'd earned fifty bucks playing guitar on the street and I gave this to Abraham, who was glad to have it.

Triple Leo

Orphaned after the black truck left town, I took to milling around the pink-and-green Venice Beach library. I knew to head there first in times of misdirection, making my way to the library, any library, like the highest point of land in a flood.

When I was a girl and my parents moved me from town to town, we sought out the library first, like a shelter. It was the first landmark we looked for.

Libraries were where I had control—I chose a book and went into it. The smells were always the same. I could slip into the cool quiet, breathe the dusty spines. Within, there was the safety of protocol, an agreed-upon civility.

A girl with a curly blond mohawk and a missing tooth sat on the front stairs, smoking a hand-rolled cigarette and getting her dog to do tricks for the passing locals in exchange for dog food.

I'd come out of the library when I heard a commotion

on the stairs, and there she was, with a circle of locals around her clapping as her little black-and-white border collie danced on its back legs. After she'd collected a few dollars and the crowd dispersed, I sat down and bummed a cigarette off her, and we spoke for a while. She had a voice worn thin from a thousand cigarettes. She introduced her dog as Bandit and herself as Jay. Bandit licked my hand and lay down at our feet. Jay told me she had a two-year-old daughter named Karma, left behind with her parents in Minnesota.

"You have a place where you sleep?" she asked me.

I told her I was looking for one.

"You can come with me. But if you tell anyone where I go at night, I'll cut yer throat."

I did not think she was lying.

Jay and I hung around that night. She bought a bottle of vodka that tasted like rusty nails, and we walked around the streets, Jay hooting and hollering and shaking her fists at tourists for fun.

When it was dark and late and I was using mailboxes and telephone poles to stay upright, Jay led me to her sleeping spot. It was a little boutique on Abbot Kinney with a white picket fence, twinkling lights in the tree branches. It was beautiful, a fairy house, off-limits to skids like us.

"*This* is where you sleep?" I asked her, leaning over the picket fence and trying not to let the vodka climb back up my throat.

The shop's white paint was purposefully peeled, made to look weather-worn. Shabbiness was an aesthetic the wealthy thought charming. There were china teapots and tin buckets of daisies on the windowsills. The little shop sold the dream of pretty things. I imagined drawing a bath in a clawfoot tub, seduced by the coziness of money.

"I don't sleep in the store, I sleep *behind* the store. There's a toolshed," said Jay, rolling her eyes at me. She looked theatrically around the boulevard but besides the lurking shapes of surfboards in shop windows and the shaggy shadows of palm trees, there was no one near. "Come on," she said and led me through the gate of the picket fence, over a pebbly path winding around the back of the shop. A little gardener's shed with a red painted door, unlocked, proved to be warm and dry. Jay pulled some burlap down from off the shelves. We spread it out on the dirt floor and slept as if we deserved to.

Carolina and I sat in the circle of palm trees. Sand blended through thin grass. From somewhere the pattering sound of a hand drum. Behind that the constant opiatic shushing of the ocean. Carolina had said something about finding some weed cookies, but as soon as we got to the beach, it was forgotten.

"My name is Daniel. Everyone calls me Leo because I am a triple Leo, astrologically speaking. That means my moon sign, my sun sign and my rising sign are all in the house of Leo."

"That's Leo," Carolina echoed to herself, staring glassily out at the line of water and sky.

"Isn't Carolina the most attractive peson on the beach?" Leo asked me. But he was the most attractive person on the beach, and he knew it. I was a fool for a pretty face. He wore floppy orange rabbit ears that hung down through his California-blond hair. He began playing pan flute, undressing me with his eyes.

"Let's go for a walk," he said. I followed him as if hypnotized, the sound of the surf pounding in my ears, the sun making my eyes heavy. The two of us strolled along the shifting sand and didn't speak because the wind whipped and blew. He grinned at me like a snake charmer, sideways, as we walked.

When we came to a toothpaste-coloured lifeguard hut, I followed him up the plank ladder and we sat in the quiet shade. He told me he was twenty-six, which seemed so much older than me. He sat close so that the edges of our fingers touched like starfish.

He said, "I was born of a Cherokee crack whore in Oregon. Evangelist Christians adopted me when I was only a baby. I fought in Afghanistan, which made my adoptive parents proud, even though all I did was guard an opium field for an American pharmaceutical company. My best friend got shot in the head by a sniper rifle during training. I watched his head explode and it looked like a watermelon being blown into pink chunks." He recited this, his blue eyes wide and sincere, as if he were trying to indoctrinate me into his church of terrible stories.

Leo told me he had been in Venice Beach for six years. "You need protecting," he said. "A Canadian girl. Already I've heard about you. You've been here, what, a couple weeks now? I heard you were the sexual plaything of Neptune and his brother. Those occult weirdos. What are you even doing here?"

I told him briefly about my pilgrimage.

He scoffed. "Only loonies come to Los Angeles on a spiritual quest. It happens all the time. These loonies come here searching and they get swallowed. They vanish. They're preyed upon. They'll follow anyone anywhere."

In the evening, I went to Abbot's Habit and asked for a cup of hot water. The man behind the counter gave me a nasty look but filled a paper cup anyway. I took it out under the awning and sat watching the passing cars, their headlights coming on slow like synthetic stars in the falling night.

Jay came around the corner, striding up to me and dragging Bandit behind her on a yellow rope. She did not say hello. "I saw you," she snarled, standing over me with her arms crossed. "Holding hands. With *Leo*." She spat his name.

"I never held his hand." I gestured for her to sit and she hesitated, not wanting to be told what to do. Finally, she sat with her legs stretched out across the sidewalk so that tourists had to step over her feet, nervously.

Jay leaned in, said confidentially, "Before he makes a sucker out of you too, I'm going to let you in on some things, little girl. Leo and I used to have a squat on Third and Rose until he got me pregnant. Did he tell you any of this? Was he talking about me?"

"No," I said.

"All right. Well. He got me pregnant. With twins, of fucking course." Jay worried the hole where her tooth had been, her angel-blue eyes fixed hard on me. "Leo is dangerous. He's a pathological liar. You'll be going along with him, sweet as you please, and that fucker will hurt you. You'll see. As soon as he found out I was knocked up, he said it wasn't his. He said I was a slut that wouldn't know who'd fixed me if my life depended on it. He wouldn't even come with me for the abortion."

"And what happened after? What did he say after you got the ..."

"Say to me?" Jay made a barking sort of laugh, but it did not reach her eyes. "He never said shit. He walks past me on the boardwalk like he doesn't even know me. But you bet he wants to ignore me. I know how tiny his dick is."

Even as she told me these things, guilt crept through me. Because I knew it was too late. Jay had given me a place to sleep, but did that make her my friend? Last night on the boardwalk she'd punched a tourist in the face just to get a few laughs. She'd turn on me too.

I saw Neptune the next day. I thought at first I was hallucinating him. He wore a pair of overalls and no shirt, his hair wild against the sky. His neck was heavy with beads and he kept running his fingers over them like he was saying a prayer.

"Neptune?" I went over. "What are you doing? Where's Kasey? Why aren't you in Texas?"

He turned his head slowly to see who was calling him— when he realized it was me, he looked away. Barely audible above the ocean and chaos of the boardwalk, he said, "The path is gonna be made clear. The path does not lead back to Texas for me." And on he went, prophesying and pointing his finger into the air as if trying to conduct electricity.

I searched the streets for the black truck. I walked up and down the boardwalk trying to find Kriel's golden head and Kasey's baby face, but they had disappeared.

I went with Leo that night. As I walked with him down the boardwalk, I saw Kriel coming toward me. She was with the drug dealer, Noah. They were holding hands, but it seemed like he was pulling her along. Kriel only nodded at me, tough in his company.

"Kriel," I called to her, and she half-turned. "I saw Neptune today ..."

"I know. They came back but now they're gone again."

"They left?" Leo tugged on my arm.

"Mhm." Noah glared at me, his eyes like a pointed gun. Kriel started to drift away with him.

"All right, well ... see you around."

"Yeah, see you."

The black truck was spotted the next day behind Abbot's Habit.

For the next week, they got as far as the highway and then changed their minds.

Kriel tried to go with them again, but they changed their minds about that too. I watched her climbing out of the truck from across the street. And she stared at me, long and hard, as if I'd done it, broken her family. I raised my hand to wave, but she only wandered off up the street.

Finally it became a joke about them leaving. Someone would say, "Kasey and Neptune decided to head back to Texas." And someone else would say back, "Guess we'll see them tonight."

Then came weeks of winter rain. The truck left for good, though I still kept my eye out for it. People came and went, things done and undone, Leo and me.

There was something about Leo that gave me a bad feeling. When he told his stories, a little voice inside me said: *What a fucking idiot, what a liar.* But some part of me liked the aversion he made me feel. It gave me power to know deep down he was a liar, a bad man. It was some kind of freedom. I had no attachment.

I ran into him somewhere along Speedway and Paloma Court in the morning, the long streets, iron bars over the windows. The low grey wool of the sky. We hadn't seen each other in a week or so. I'd been avoiding him, and I think he knew it. He stopped walking and I stopped walking. He had a mean expression on his face. I watched a seagull tear apart a big clear chunk of gristle.

"What's new then?"

"What's new?" he echoed. "What's new, what's new ..." He was savouring something, a diamond of gossip that hadn't reached me yet. He had the wide, cold, clear eyes of a crazy person. "Neptune's dead. He killed himself." And when he saw my face, he smiled, relishing my reaction. "You didn't hear?"

I leaned against the building.

"His immigrant brother went to all the trouble of getting his crazy ass back to Texas and as soon as they get there, he up and kills himself. Go figure."

The rain came down on my face. I turned and ran down the alley. My toes slipped and slid in my shoes. I went swift and silent through the streets, any streets, it didn't matter where I was, I didn't know. Neptune was supposed to be with his daughter and wife. His brother. He was supposed to make it home.

From behind me Leo called my name, laughing at my back until I could no longer hear him, his voice swallowed by the labyrinth of leaning buildings.

The streets opened up on the beach, waves of curling concrete crashed. The endless slate of sea. And the seagulls screamed as the wind tore them from the sky, throwing them toward the dirt like used napkins.

I found Kriel standing alone under a palm tree. I went to her side and neither of us said a word.

I had a bus ticket back to Canada.

"But you're not going," Leo told me. "What do you have to go back to?"

How far I had come to outrun my family, the ugly box house in the rural backwoods of Nova Scotia. Waiting behind me were the brown snow and the hard, empty landscape. I had sought out people like myself and found solidarity in their trash-picking and war stories, and in that way had built my own home from the scraps piled around me.

I thought of the pilgrimage that had brought me to California in the first place, the forgotten ashram, the temple I wasn't ready for. Maybe I was still on the path to transformation. I couldn't tell. Every day I woke up and was thrown so hard into the hours I didn't think about moving forward or back. I couldn't think that far ahead—it would dull the edge of my senses and I needed them sharp.

Sitting in front of the coffee shop in the California sun, surrounded by smiling transients as arrested in their development as myself, counting quarters for a cup of coffee, there wasn't anywhere else to go. I had arrived.

I threw my bus ticket in a trash can on the way down to the beach.

Sleeping on the beach was not as romantic as it sounded. In fact, it was the most dangerous place to lay your head. I had only slept on the beach once, with Kriel. When you were out on the sand, you were completely exposed to whoever might find you. Usually it was police. They swept the beach at night, beating and arresting anyone stupid enough to fall asleep in plain view. I had been sleeping in the Venice Beach library parking lot under a hedgerow with a switchblade. But a group of men had spotted me and began to yell and holler. I'd waited for them to leave, tense and holding my knife. They walked on but I spent the night with my eyes open, knowing I'd need to find another spot.

Leo was batshit crazy and this craziness protected me. I went with him at night, on the scrounge for places to sleep. He knew every weirdo on the boardwalk. The more riddled with tics and bad behaviour, the more probable it was they ran around with Leo.

Like Craig. A bloated alcoholic in his mid-forties, he let us sleep in the spare room of his apartment sometimes. The floor had a carpet, so we threw blankets in the corner and curled up. The only furniture in the boxy rooms was a kitchen chair and a big-screen television. Craig stumbled home in the early hours and fell face down on the floor. He had to walk everywhere because his car had been impounded.

One morning, Leo and I were walking down the alley behind Abbot Kinney and found a garbage bag with freshly laundered blankets inside. Someone must have put it out for people such as ourselves. Nearby, we found a swath of new cardboard. We bundled all of this up and hid it for later that night. When it got dark, we came and grabbed it, setting up a bed in the corner of the library parking lot under the sweep of a cottonwood tree.

The nights before, we'd been sleeping by the canals behind a dumpster. But there were knife fights down under the bridge where people never slept and slashed at anything that came too close, blasting their stereo music and screaming long into the night. The only good thing about being behind the dumpster was that we'd found a shopping cart. It had been floating half in the canal water, lacy with weeds and chunky with rust. There were only three working wheels on it, but Leo said a shopping cart was a valuable commodity. When we found the bedding, we packed up our bedroom and pushed it away in the cart.

On the boardwalk, I saw Alex and his girlfriend, Izzy, her dark hair hanging in bunches. She said she was from Israel, and the nickname was a logical extension. I had no idea what her real name was, but I was getting used to that.

When Alex and Izzy saw me, they laughed and called me a *home bum.* I didn't know what that meant.

"Look," said Alex. He pointed at an old man slouching past, grey hair flattened to his skull. The man carried a plastic bag full of rattling cans along the ridge of his spine. "That's a home bum. You know where he's headed right now? To get his shopping cart. He's gonna put his cans in it and roll it around. He's probably only got a good five years left. And you know where he's going to spend 'em? Right here doing the same exact shit." Alex came from New Hampshire and sneered at anyone who stayed in one place for longer than two weeks.

The others were also defiantly proud of their wandering. They refused to go easy. Leo's bed and shopping cart, and everything else Leo did, was part of something they didn't want and couldn't understand. I wondered if I was making the wrong choice, going around with him, but I didn't trust myself to go it alone.

The sun woke me up like a shining alarm clock at six a.m., morning after morning. The smells came first: the asphalt, the cottonwood tree, a hand-rolled cigarette coming from somewhere, the salt of the ocean, the oil of the cars.

The parking lot was full of people sleeping in the painted spaces, rolled up in their ratty blankets.

Leo sold pot and as soon as the travellers woke, they made their way over to our cardboard bed to get some. Scavenging was respected and any commodity was obtained by bartering. In exchange for weed, Leo and I received clean socks, oranges, dental floss, cans of beer, cigarettes, paperback books or pens.

One morning, I opened my eyes and a teenager was sitting there waiting for us to wake up. I only knew him from seeing him around. His name was Twist. Twist's black hair hung across his round brown face in messy curls. He said he was eighteen but that was probably a lie. He bragged about his mom's place in East LA, her medicine cabinet full of pills. He'd been dubbed Twist because he wore a little green cap and a long coat, like a Latino Oliver Twist.

He sat there polite and quiet until I got up, and then he asked me if he could trade some tea bags or food stamps for a gram of Leo's weed.

On the day I met Half-Peach for the very first time, they were standing in a pay phone booth to keep their straw hat dry. They had a banjo on their back and kept jauntily snapping their suspenders.

They were with Alex and a spaced-out girl named Connie. Connie didn't wear shoes. Her feet were bright pink, her jeans sagged down over her concave pelvis, and she stood there chattering in a little T-shirt. She'd hacked her straw-coloured hair off and her freckled cheeks were whipped red from the cold wind. Her eyes were upturned to the sky like a supplicant. I saw her around on that day with Half-Peach and a few times after that. Then she vanished completely. People went looking for her, but we never saw her again.

"I met them in Illinois," said Alex, indicating his huckleberry friend. "You got into town when, yesterday?"

"That's right," Half-Peach said, nodding. They picked up the phone and pressed it to their ear to see if it worked.

"I'm waiting for someone," I said to explain my being there, though that wasn't necessary. All we ever did was hang around.

Leo was up in Pacific Palisades. One of his friends had offered us a place to sleep during the rains, which were supposed to come steady for the next two weeks. This friend was one Jeffrey, a Muscle Beach regular. Jeffrey was supposed to pick Leo and me up on the corner in his car, but Leo hadn't shown up and Jeffrey was late anyway.

So I hung around the phone booth with Half-Peach, letting them charm me with their song and dance. Trying not to think about Leo and the bad taste he was leaving in my mouth. I felt as if I were slowly breaking off from the land and slipping into the sea.

Daniel

The mansion had no lights. The entire property was fenced in against the hill, spiky green plants bursting over the wooden slats.

Jeffrey said Dill, the man who owned the house, was a tweaker—he did crystal meth. But he was a wealthy tweaker, which had led to full-blown gadget madness and raging galactic nights, crashes and abundant toolboxes.

Jeffrey lived in a little cottage behind the house in a concrete courtyard. He'd sold a screenplay for two million bucks and moved in with Dill. "He needed someone to help him get organized," was how Jeffrey put it.

Jeffrey's bedspread was leopard print, the walls painted red, mirrors on the ceiling. And on the night Leo and I arrived, there was also a girl.

She was riled up as a house cat left out in the rain. Jeffrey said he had *found her* but wouldn't elaborate. Her name was Jessica and she paced the cottage, reading her poetry aloud from a piece of scrap paper doodled with flowers and hearts. She didn't notice we were in the room until she finished reading. When she did finally look up, her eyes glittering behind a pair of plastic glasses, she did not see us but instead stared at the space above our heads as if there was something floating there.

Dill came back to the cottage to meet us. He had on an ugly sweater, his hands shook, his glasses slid down his nose. Jeffrey was halfway through a bottle of syrupy wine, his teeth stained grey with it. In the corner of the cottage was an electric keyboard, and after saying a clipped hello, Dill sat at the instrument, running his fingers over complex, watery melodies. I sat stiffly on the edge of Jeffrey's bed.

When Dill went back into the house, Jessica grabbed Jeffrey by the arm and pulled him outside, where I could hear them having words. He muttered under his breath, but her dialogue was bright and splashy with emotion. Something about how she wanted to go home, how she hadn't been understood. Leo cleared his throat at me and made a spinning gesture with his finger near his ear, to indicate Jessica was insane. He'd set up our sleeping bags already and was just climbing into his when Jeffrey came crashing back into the cottage, harassed.

Jessica stayed outside in the rain. From the windows I could see her dancing around, dripping wet, waving her arms over her head like a crazy palm tree, as manic as if she'd been hit by lightning.

Jeffrey rolled his eyes. He sat on the end of his bed,

elbows on his knees. He didn't say anything about the present drama but said instead, "I know Dill seems like an interesting person, but don't let your guard down." He was looking at me. "He's a common drug addict. He's got some young thug living with him in the house, probably his dealer."

"What's with Jessica?" Leo finally asked as she waltzed past the door.

"I fucked her," Jeffrey confessed. "But now I don't know what to do with her. She's a runaway I think, I don't know. I have to get her out of here." And then he finally noticed our sleeping bags and said, "Grab your stuff. Dill said you can have a room in the house."

I felt a wash of secret relief that we wouldn't have to be out in the cottage with Jeffrey and the teenaged girl.

He led us through the double doors at the back of the mansion, the floors icy underfoot. There were piles and piles of stuff in the corners of the vaulted kitchen, sheaths of plastic and picked-apart metal and tin, the counters piled with plates, power tools all over the floor. It was a den of screws, a factory of wires and radio parts.

The kitchen had one light, wavering like the sanity inside the house. It looked and smelled like a fish tank. The attached living room had a lone chair and the carpet, once white, had gone grey with filth. Dill was nowhere to be found, but digital noises emanated from the depths of the house.

Jeffrey led us down a hallway. "This is where that young thug lives," he whispered. I could just make out the dome of Jeffrey's head in the shadows. "Keep an eye on your belongings. That gangster will steal them, or Dill will try and take them apart. This used to be a beautiful house. Now look at it. He's got enough money he could hire a fucking housekeeper. Whatever. Lock your door behind you." And Jeffrey disappeared back down the hall.

Leo was unperturbed by this new information. He was always talking about how he used to be a tweaker, bragging about his addiction as if he had earned a degree.

When we entered the bedroom and turned on the light, I gasped. The only piece of furniture was a mattress in the middle of the floor. The entire back wall, from floor to fifteen-foot ceiling, was heaped with machinery. Old speakers, buttons and plastic, VCRs, car stereos, computer towers. And all of it had been dissected. The plastic and steel and copper wire pressed tight against the ceiling, digging into the plaster.

"Oh my god," I whispered.

There was a knock on the door.

"Don't you dare answer it," Leo commanded.

I ignored him. It was the nameless gangster. He was ashen faced, his eyes like pale stars. He wore a baggy velour suit, his head shaved down to the skin. He walked into the room and sat on the floor cross-legged.

"You friends of Jeffrey's?" His voice was guttural. He couldn't have been older than us, but his face was heavier.

"Yeah," I answered.

Leo left the room in a huff.

"My name's Rochester," he said, holding out a hand for me to shake.

"Thanks for letting us crash here," I told him.

"Ain't my house. It's Dill's. He's fucked up, but he's all right. You mind?" Rochester took out a thin glass pipe and a plastic baggy packed with what looked like shards of glass. He didn't wait for me to say anything. Sprinkling the glass into the bowl, he held up the flame of his lighter and let it cook the contents of the pipe until a white smoke pooled. He pulled hard on it, leaning his head back against the wall. Closed his eyes as if I weren't there anymore.

Leo came back a few minutes later and fell into bed, asleep or pretending to be. Not long after that, Rochester gave me a salute and stood unsteadily, turning off the light and closing the door behind him.

In the night I had to use the bathroom. The robot noises were still coming from somewhere in the unknowable house.

The bathroom was a few doors down the hallway, and when I went in and turned on the blueish light, I saw the walls and ceiling had been papered in old maps—turquoise water, orange and pink land masses with names like Zaire, Burma, Czechoslovakia, Ceylon, Prussia, Yugoslavia.

I was about to go back to my room when I heard screaming from the courtyard, a primal wailing followed by shouts. I hesitated with my hand on the knob, waiting to see if Dill or Rochester would come running, if Leo would wake up. But nothing happened. No one came.

I slipped back down the dark hall into the bedroom and locked the door.

The next morning, Jeffrey made us breakfast in his cottage. He said he'd kicked Jessica out in the night. "Things got ugly" was all he would say as he fried us eggs on a hot plate.

I missed the sprawl of the beach, the warmth of Venice and the familiarity of the routines there. But it was still raining.

When the rain finally stopped that afternoon, it was just in time. Jeffrey had asked Leo if he was interested in loaning me to him. I told Leo to pack up our things. We would walk back to the beach.

I went into the house to thank Dill for his hospitality, but he was nowhere to be found. Instead I found Rochester, sitting in the living room chair, staring at the carpet. His eyes two red spiderwebs.

"You outta here?" he mumbled, staring intently at his feet.

"Yeah, we're heading back to Venice Beach," I said.

Rochester made no indication he'd heard me. He began picking frantically at the lint on his pants. "Fuck, I gotta get some sleep," he said. "It's been days."

Down through the hills, tsunami warning signs peppered the streets. The trees were dense and wild, orange blossoms bursting from the foliage. Everything lush and jungly from the days of rain. A humid wash rose up from the shimmering pavement, the air clean and sparkling. I ran with relief down the road. I would find the others on the boardwalk, our little gang, Izzy, Twist, and Alex. I felt a surge of excitement when I thought of Half-Peach. I would straighten up. I would guard myself. I would get away from Leo. I too could be washed clean.

When we reached the beaches down on the lip of Pacific Palisades, we saw three older home bums camping on the sand. Two men with steel wool beards and baseball caps sitting cross-legged with a lady, her hair in grey-brown pigtails, wearing sneakers and a flowered dress. They told us their names, which were so ridiculous they didn't stick, and offered Leo and me some rum and orange juice. The morning sun was bright, but the air was cold.

"You know it's better in Venice Beach," said Leo.

The woman scoffed. "Pacific Palisades is nice and quiet. We can sit here all gawd-dang morning and drink our juice. No young gangbangers trying to stab us and no LAPD threatening to drag us away. At night we curl up, see that cliff right over there? We curl up just there. It's nice and quiet."

It was my fault for letting my sense pleasures ensnare me. I returned to the book. I read the stories of miracles and magic and felt ashamed I'd been seduced, by the city and by men. What would the German nun think of me? This couldn't have been what I'd needed to see in order to satisfy my worldly desire. It didn't feel big enough.

It had been Leo's idea to go to Pacific Palisades in the first place. As we walked back to the boardwalk, he told me his big plans for us, where we would sleep, hustles we needed to do together. I remembered Jay and the abortion—some quiet part of myself warned me to back away slowly, before something happened that I couldn't undo.

In the coming weeks, all I knew of Leo's presence were rumours: He'd gone to a marijuana farm. He'd shipped out with the navy. He'd found a woman to adopt him in Laurel Canyon. He'd left town completely. I'd broken his heart.

The days were hard and cold and lonely. Jay and Alex coupled up and went off somewhere together; Half-Peach was in Humboldt County. And I was sleeping alone again. When I ran into Leo behind Big Daddy's, he told me he'd been a mess without me, that he was in love with me and crazy about it. When I measured my loneliness against my desire for spiritual transformation, one was tangible and the other was not. The only cure for the pain of life seemed to be clinging to another human. Where was God? I hadn't seen him.

Leo's latest scheme was the old Alcoholics Anonymous hustle. You showed up, said you were a drunk and they gave you free coffee and donuts. Sometimes even a place to sleep.

The meeting that night was in a rented hall in Santa Monica. Leo and I mingled with the hopeful ex-drinkers and met a man named Andrew, a computer programmer with a house in Malibu.

While we lingered around the fold-out table with its plastic tablecloth and Styrofoam coffee cups, Andrew told us about a big sober party he'd thrown at his house. "It was wild, DJs and celebrities. A lot of stars are trying sobriety."

Leo said, "Bet you have extra room at your place."

I sipped my stale coffee, embarrassed by Leo's begging. Paramahansa Yogananda never had to beg. But I had chosen men instead of God.

"The property is a real mess right now, energy drink cans and garbage everywhere," said Andrew, looking restlessly over his shoulder. People were starting to sit down in the aluminum chairs. A speaker cleared his throat from behind the podium. "But tell you what. If you come clean up for me, I'll let you stay in the pool house."

After the meeting, we climbed in the back of Andrew's car and drove through the dark hills, the warm safety of the back seat like a lit-up cave. Leo sat in the front seat and Little Wing, curled inside my shirt, made snuffly snoring noises, the peace of a sleeping pup. She had it easy.

As we drove, Andrew asked us what kinds of foods we liked. I was so used to eating whatever I could get that I'd lost any preference. What did I like to eat? I didn't know. Leo was already listing his favourite meals and snacks. "There's a fridge in the pool house," Andrew said. "Might as well fill it up."

He hadn't been lying about the energy drink cans and the garbage. Andrew parked the car in the driveway and led us up the hill behind his sprawling mansion to the pool. The hills were dense with avocado trees, a crumbling set of stairs disappearing into the darkness of the foliage. "I found a bunker up there when I moved in." Andrew pointed into the depths of the jungle.

"I will have to check that out," said Leo gleefully.

The lawn was messy with sodden streamers and wilted balloons, tree branches blown to the ground from the heavy rain. Andrew handed us garbage bags. "It's late and dark," he said. "Get some rest and don't worry about tackling anything until tomorrow morning." He said goodnight and vanished down the path to the house.

"I can't believe we have to clean this trash," Leo said when Andrew was gone. "Just like a rich person, recruiting someone else to clean his filth."

I pretended I didn't hear him and unrolled my sleeping bag on the floor of the empty pool house.

"Nobody knows what I've been through this week," Leo griped. He sat on the lip of the pool and dangled his legs in the turquoise water.

I picked up a syringe from the grass. "I wonder if Andrew knows how sober his parties are."

After I had finished picking up the garbage from the wet grass, Andrew let us come down to the house. While he played video games with Leo on a television that took up his entire wall, I had a bath in a sunken tub, making the water as hot as I could stand. Every luxury felt scarce and one-of-a-kind.

In the steaming hot morning light, I closed my eyes and felt the liquid chuckling and pressing on my body; alone with the metronomic drips and splashes, I closed my eyes, was anywhere.

What if every day was like this one, a running through the hours, a grasping, a corporeal exhaustion, scrambling after sensual needs? I felt the physical pull to only chase dreams with pleasure. But what would happen to me when my breath wound down? I thought about it at night, in the dark, when I pulled the blankets over my face to shut out the street lights and the noise of the city. I wasn't afraid of the other side of life, the infinity outside this human holding cell, but I feared the transition. That fear crept into the soft edges of my daily life. It came crawling like smoke, into my wide-awake brain, the brightness of light shining on the slinking curiosity of what would happen to me. What was supposed to happen to me.

After my bath, Andrew took us with him to an AA meeting. He went to one every day. The meeting was in Hollywood, held in a building that looked like a ski lodge. The rain had turned the sky to grey paper.

The lodge was crammed with washed-up actors I recognized from television shows, their faces sheepish.

When everyone settled in their seats, the crowd was encouraged to stand up one by one and declare their allegiance to an alcoholic identity. Leo said, "My name's Daniel and I'm an alcoholic." Everyone mumbled back, "Hi, Daniel." I'd never witnessed Leo take a drink in all the time I'd known him. I would not stand.

Usually with the AA meetings, there was a special speaker who'd regale the crowd with their testimony, a long, sordid account of every crime committed while under alcohol's influence. Today's speaker was a flamboyant man not much older than me. He gave us the standard greeting: "My name's Facundo and I'm an alcoholic." "Hi, Facundo," we all said back. And then he began reciting his personal grocery list of bad behaviours while drunk, finally playing his trump card: "I knew things had gotten *truly* out of hand when I woke up one morning hog-tied in the closet." He hung his head sadly. "It didn't matter whose dick it was, I would suck it. I drank so much that my esophagus tore open from drinking and puking. Felt like a chunk of un-swallowed meat at the back of my throat." He gripped the pulpit with sincerity, appealing to us with liquid eyes to save ourselves before it was too late. I ducked my chin and slowly turned my head to the side. Leo sat there with tears rolling down his cheeks. Andrew had his arm around his shoulders. They made salvation look so easy.

During the long days when Andrew was at work, Leo wanted to attend meetings in Culver City.

"But we have food and shelter at Andrew's. What do you want to go to extra meetings for?" Although I had heard the Culver City meetings had the best donuts and coffee. I'd also become worried about wearing out our welcome at Andrew's. He came home at night exhausted. He wasn't running a homeless shelter. What did he owe us? Old anxieties rose up. That same panicked helplessness. Sleeping on my sister's couch, growing up in my parents' house. The fact of my presence. When Leo said we should strike out on our own for a few days, I went with him.

Leo was certainly addicted, but it wasn't drugs or alcohol he craved—it was the meetings themselves. He started getting everyone to call him Daniel, the name on his birth certificate. He wanted to prove he wasn't the same man who played pan flute and danced around the sand wearing rabbit ears, but I wasn't sure who he was trying to prove it *to*. The meetings underscored the dysfunction of his personality. Once he told me he'd masturbated until his dick bled. When people gave him food, he shoved it into his mouth all at once, theatrically, like a man who hadn't eaten in years, choking, his eyes watering.

I went with him anyway, redacting the parts that irked me. I was as unsure of myself and my own mind as he was of his. He chose meetings as a remedy. And I chose him.

We spent the next three days in Culver City, sleeping in a stairwell at night.

One of the regulars at the Culver City meetings was a man named Hank. Hank had hair dyed half-orange and half-black, and had the face of a cartoon character: long drooping nose, bulgy darting eyes. His teeth were eaten away by crystal meth, eroded down to broken brown spikes.

On the first day, he told us he would be our sponsor and help us study the Book.

Hank also sponsored a man named Joe. I'd seen Joe around Venice Beach before, getting into all sorts of drunken trouble. He wore the same pair of denim overalls every day and always spoke with awe about everything, as if he were seeing it all for the first time. Joe was in his forties, but he had the lit-up face of a child and was as hyper as one, shouting himself constantly into a state of mania and then falling asleep during meetings. I egged him on by laughing at his antics. Leo and Hank did not approve of either of us. I was not what I, or anyone else, would consider an alcoholic, and Joe refused to admit that being an alcoholic wasn't fun.

Between meetings Joe and I went to the parking lot of the 99 Cent Store and put a hat down at our feet. The sun had spent the whole day heating the asphalt, and in the evening, the waves of warmth came up to meet my face. I was like a lizard chasing the light, baked into ambivalence. When Joe and I had earned almost ten bucks, we walked across the highway to a Mexican restaurant and got tacos, Leo and Hank watching us from the steps of the meeting hall, the Book open on their laps.

The stairwell above the meeting hall was as good a place to sleep as any. There was no foot traffic at night, and we were closed off from the street. The night before, there'd been a cop poking around, but we lay still and made ourselves look like a pile of garbage until he went away again. That was a trick Leo had taught me, to bundle myself up so that I didn't resemble a body at all.

In the morning, we woke at six in the grainy light and went down the stairs to catch the first meeting of the day. There was fresh coffee and, the rumours were true, the best donuts in town. If the AA patrons realized we were sleeping on the stairs above them, they never said. Besides, we weren't the only ones with a grubby, repentant aura.

Hank came to the meeting at ten and afterwards took us to a park so we could read "Bill's Story." Hank said he had the whole Book memorized and quoted it frequently as proof. We sat at a picnic table, the sky a watery white, my shoes damp, the air chilly. I pulled my sweater around me. I missed having a place to live on days like this, when all I wanted to do was curl up somewhere and drink tea and be warm. Having no place to go, if you thought about it too long, could choke the air out of you. There were steps: Go to a shelter. Get a minimum wage job. Save paycheques. Maybe get a roommate. Try to run, catch up.

Hank had just reached the part where Bill starts playing golf with bankers and working on his tan when it began to rain. "Let's go," he said, jumping to his feet and holding his arms over his head. Leo stuffed the Book under his shirt to keep it dry. We ran across the green, following Hank to a dirt lot where a few trailers were parked.

"This is me," Hank said, leading us up stairs carpeted in Astroturf. "Emmy?" he called as he ducked through the trailer door.

There was a smell of stale perfume. I slipped out of my sodden shoes and walked on tiptoe across the carpet. The light was blocked out by burgundy curtains over the windows. Mason jars of ostrich feathers stood on upside-down milk crates covered with silk scarves and ragged lace. Hung on the walls in place of photographs were old dresses.

"That you, Hank?" A voice trembled from the end of the house.

"Sit down, sit down," Hank said, and Leo and I sunk into the depths of a velvet couch. Leo wore the same blank expression I did. We had become so accustomed to being pulled this way and that, winding up anywhere, seeing anything. As soon as I sat, a stiff little poodle hopped up beside me and fell, stinking, into my lap.

"Get that thing out of here," Leo said, but Little Wing climbed out of my shirt to meet the poodle and the two of them began wrestling on the sofa.

Hank had gone off to find whoever Emmy was and now came lumbering back, followed by a tiny blue-haired old woman. "This is my landlady, Emmy," he said, lurching and ducking through the trailer to the kitchen. "I'm making us tea," he called over his shoulder.

Emmy sat in the armchair across from us and smiled. Her lipstick had gone into the cracks of her mouth and made little red stitches, like a rag doll. Her veiny hands looked like bundles of blue yarn, a papery covering of skin. "I'm not just his landlady," she said. "I'm also his friend. I used to have many friends." Her voice was thin as bone china. "Would you like to see some photographs?"

"Not really." Leo yawned and headed into the kitchen to find Hank.

"Oh." Emmy blinked very hard.

"Don't mind him, he's an alcoholic," I said to Emmy. "Come sit here." I patted Leo's empty seat. "I would love to see some photographs." I remembered long afternoons at my grandmother's, turning page after page of pictures sheathed in plastic. It had been a way to speak to one another, picking out the memories that had been good, and so were photographed.

Emmy opened the book to the beginning. The sepia photos showed her rich with youth. Waving in front of the Hollywood sign, grinning in lipstick, plastic pearls, white gloves. "Wasn't I something?" she said, clucking her tongue and tracing her fingertip over the lost version of her face. "I used to be friends with Katharine Hepburn."

"Your dresses are beautiful," I said covetously.

"I still wear them to the grocery store. Never know who you're going to see in Los Angeles! This used to be a magical place." Emmy looked down at her hands as if she were trying to make sense of them, ravaged as they were by age.

Leo walked through the living room carrying two mugs of steaming tea.

"For us, dear?" Emmy asked.

"No. Hank and I are going to his room to read 'Bill's story.'" And he continued down the hall.

Hank came after him. "Emmy, it's almost two. Deb said she's picking you up for your appointment, remember? Better go wait for her outside so you don't get left again."

"That's right," said Emmy.

"C'mon with us," Hank said to me. I followed him down the low-ceilinged hall to his bedroom. Behind me, I heard the front door open and close.

Leo was already situated on the end of the bed, slurping his tea. Hank used a sleeping bag as a blanket, which made me think that not too long ago, he'd been sleeping outside as we did. The room smelled of old socks and unwashed body.

"I know," said Hank when he caught me looking at the dirty clothes on the floor.

"Can we get on with it?" Leo said, flipping open the leather-bound volume. "Bill's life is about to go all to hell."

The next day we were back at Andrew's. Leo was lying poolside in the early morning, bragging about the military's positive influence in the Middle East. Leo had a way of speechifying that didn't require a listener. I was used to tuning him out, letting other people rise to his contrarianism. But now we were alone.

I sat on a cold plastic pool chair, smoking a cigarette and watching Little Wing roll in the grass, trying to find the weak sun. I ignored Leo's nattering until he brought up Neptune.

"The world has no place for mental retards like that, see. The warden should have never released him from jail—people like him were made for prison. They can't help being a statistic. Of course he killed himself. There was nothing else he could have done."

The cigarette fell from my fingers. "You need to shut the fuck up now."

"No way," Leo said, as indifferently as if he were speaking of the weather.

I was on my feet. I saw Neptune's face, gentle in the night, that first night. I'd been cozying up with a Judas and I'd known it from the minute I went with Leo. "There's something wrong with you," I said to him. As if I could convince him. He radiated something so deeply broken that it pulled me in, a black hole, an absence of light. My hands formed fists.

Leo grabbed Little Wing. He jumped up, pushing me

out of his way, and moved to the edge of the pool. He had her by the scruff of her neck, holding her over the water. "I will drown this rat," he said. Little Wing whimpered and pedalled the air with her tiny paws.

"Give me my dog," I said, my throat closing up. I moved toward him and yet away, trying to reach for her but trying not to push him. I knew he would do it.

And then he let go.

I grabbed her as she fell toward the water. And when she was in my arms, a warm bundle, I held her tight. But the snatch of security was gone again as Leo kicked out my ankles. I flipped onto the cement, the wind knocked out of me. Little Wing tossed to the grass.

"You're as mentally unhinged as that gorilla." He stood over me, his face obliterated by the sun.

I lay there gasping. Leo let me get to my feet and then he grabbed me again. It was like being held by a machine. He dragged me into the pool house. I wanted to scream, but there wasn't enough air or time.

He slammed the door behind us and barred it with his body. "I see I can't trust you," he said. He put his hand on his pocket, where he carried his switchblade. "I'm missing some things. I had some money and some belongings. They're gone. What did you do with them?"

"What?" I tried to rush the door, but he shoved me back hard and I fell against the wall. Little Wing cried from outside, her nails scraping the door.

"Don't fucking tell me "what," you cunt. You fucking ran around with that crew of hippies. I was right not to trust you."

"I didn't take your shit? What are you talking about?"

But Leo held his pocket. "If you didn't steal from me, prove it. Show me your bag."

"I just wanna leave," I said. I tried to keep my voice neutral so he wouldn't come after me again.

In my mind, I could see the driveway and the road, the route back to the beach. Everything had been there a minute ago. Now there were only the walls of the pool house.

When Leo saw my bag on the floor and went toward it, I tried to get past him.

He was waiting for that. He grabbed my neck and squeezed. My body was so puny. "You dumb bitch." He threw me back against the wall.

But when he crouched down to pick up my bag, I charged the door again, scooped up Little Wing and shoved her inside my shirt. I ran, a bundle of jangling limbs.

I heard him yelling, his shoes hitting the gravel. But I was faster. I got to Andrew's door, throwing myself into it, hitting the glass with my fists.

He came out groggy and irritated, then alarmed when he understood, Leo running onto the deck.

"Please take me back to the beach," I said.

Leo came up behind me, grabbing my arm and twisting it silently. My elbow creaked.

"Hey now," Andrew said. "Everything okay? Let her go, there."

Leo dropped my arm and stepped back. "So dramatic," he muttered. "She's having some kind of episode."

"Can you just take me back to the beach?" I said to Andrew.

"Why don't you come inside," he said to me. "Leo, can you wait out here? If you need a ride anywhere, I'll call my girlfriend."

"I don't want to put you out, man," Leo said casually. "I'll ride down to the beach with you both."

"I said wait here." Andrew reached out for my shoulder and brought me inside. Slid the door shut behind me, locked it. "What happened to your neck? Do I need to call the cops?"

"No cops. Just take me back to Venice." I sat on the floor and held Little Wing against my chest, my external heart. I could make it up the mountain to the temple once more. I'd go back to the water and start again.

Andrew paced the room, tied his robe tighter. Rubbed the stubble along his jaw. "I need to get that person out of my pool house," he muttered to himself. Then to me, "Do you have your things?"

"In the pool house..." My guitar bag. The book. A sweater. A notebook. A pen. Everything I owned in the world.

"I'll get them. You wait here. Keep the door locked. Are you sure you want to go back to the beach? Will you be all right?"

"I'll be just fine," I said.

He dropped me off on Abbot Kinney and I walked down to the boardwalk. He'd asked Leo to leave and we watched him walk down the road before getting in the car and heading out.

The gang was sitting behind Bench Lady's bench, one of our meeting spots on the boardwalk. There they were, sprawled on the grass as if I'd never left.

I tried to make kin out of anyone I came across because I was so far away from blood relatives. If we got drunk together more than a couple times, they were family. If they loaned me five bucks or listened to my melodrama, they became my brother. It fooled me into thinking some unbreakable bond had formed through our shared loneliness. I sat down in their midst, Twist, Jay, Half-Peach, Izzy, Alex, and told them what had happened up in Malibu. They were outraged but not surprised. Jay, her blue eyes still and silent, did not say I told you so. She did not say anything at all.

Christmas in Venice Beach

There was no better time to be homeless in Los Angeles than at Christmas. Leading up to the day, I stopped buying toothbrushes and tampons and deodorant. I waited. Everyone in the neighbourhood did.

On Christmas morning we came out of our hiding spots, blinking in the winter sun. On the basketball courts, volunteers from a Baptist church unfolded tables. A crowd gathered. Old men, still drunk, propped themselves up against their shopping carts. Teenagers high on acid, their eyes like light bulbs, pit bulls straining on leashes, their fur gleaming in the early morning light.

The congregation wore matching orange T-shirts with the name of their church emblazoned in yellow letters. They passed around Styrofoam plates heavy with food. Travel-sized toothbrushes and little deodorants in plastic baggies like a dope deal. They dumped big piles of clothes on the ground with the idea that we should pick through them. Seagulls pinwheeled above the basketball courts, diving for dropped food.

I stood off to the side, eating quietly from a plate of potatoes and canned cranberries. I turned down turkey three times from the church people walking by with tinfoil trays. "I don't eat anything that had a mother," I said. I was spoiled to have any kind of standard on the street, but I hung on to little things.

Leo saw I was alone and came over, smoking a menthol cigarette, the orange rabbit ears hanging down over his sun-bleached hair. He was so handsome and psychotic that I had to look away. "Some rich producer is handing out hundred-dollar bills," he said. "He's on a street corner somewhere between the Santa Monica Pier and Muscle Beach." And then he went off across the parking lot. I didn't follow him.

I'd bought myself some Christmas cigarettes from Henry's Market and was on my way to meet Kriel behind Bench Lady's bench when someone called out to me.

"Hey girly. Girly." It was Tony. He manned a booth on the boardwalk called Heaven's Pennies. Heaven's Pennies was some kind of soup kitchen, nothing more than a folding table and a tarp. In his mid-forties, gold chains around his thick neck, Tony hailed from Mar Vista. When he wasn't running Heaven's Pennies, he could be seen roaring around the streets of Venice Beach in his busted-up white truck, going to AA meetings at any hour of the day.

Tony kept the back of his truck loaded down with a crusty black cooking pot, plastic ladles, bushels of wilting vegetables, bags of stale buns and crates upon crates of ramen noodles from the 99 Cent Store. He'd come walking along the boardwalk like the Pied Piper, followed by a pack of drunk punks and hippie kids.

Tony set up shop anywhere he could find space on the boardwalk: beside sunglasses stands or people with sandwich boards advertising *Medical Grade Marijuana*; dreadlocked women behind tables loaded down with crystals; hip-hop artists holding up their jeans with one hand and selling their homemade CDs with the other. Every morning around six or seven, Tony squeezed his table into the boardwalk's barrage and began making his free soup, turning on the hot plate hooked up to his rattling generator. Tony dumped whatever he could find into his soup: raisins, cherry tomatoes, cinnamon, celery. It all went in, bubbling up with an odour of scorched salt and starch. During the crowded afternoons on the boulevard, locals and drifters were united by their dripping Styrofoam cups.

Tony smoked menthol cigarettes so nobody would bum them. He called out to everyone who walked the boardwalk, celebrities, tourists, punks on skateboards, "Free soup! Made by the grace of God." More often than not, Tony set up the table and then recruited someone from the boardwalk to guard it while he went to meet his sponsor.

That Christmas Day, he'd made a sign from a piece of cardboard and drew coins with wings all over it with a black marker.

I could smell the boiling soup before I'd even reached the table. Behind the boardwalk lay the cold dampness of the sand, the waves making a soft *shhhhhh*ing noise. The palm trees hung down like old curtains and the pink afternoon sun painted itself slowly across the dome of space.

Men were always calling to me on the boardwalk. I had trained myself to keep my eyes focused ahead. I didn't want to get involved in whatever Tony wanted me to be involved in, but Christmas fooled me into a sense of obligation.

"Wanna watch the table?" Tony asked me.

He was gone three hours. I kept the soup going, and a woman named Lisa who'd grown up with Tony in South Central came along to help me dish up cups and pass them around.

Heaven's Pennies usually gathered a crowd: hangers-on, locals and hippies. An actor from an old detective show brought down a couple garbage bags full of clothes and stuffed animals and colouring books and dumped the contents on the ground. Curious tourists gathered, wanting him to write his name on their stomachs, arms, old socks, lunch boxes, and then dispersed again, a school of colourful fish flitting around the boardwalk.

Lisa knelt, extracting mittens and hats from the actor's garbage bags and passing them around, even though the winter day was warm. I left the pot of soup and went over to help her.

"Good holiday?" she asked me. Lisa had one of Tony's menthols hanging out of the corner of her mouth. The smoke softened the hardness of her face. She wore men's pants and a denim shirt, a long braid of hair hanging down her back. Lisa said things simply and she wanted the same given back to her, plain-speak and respect. This made her easy to talk to.

"Good enough," I said.

"Christmas got too much to live up to," said Lisa, flicking her smoke out at the water.

A group of hippies passed by, shouting about the producer's hundred-dollar-bill giveaway. The holy man had been seen on Third and Rose. Someone else said he'd been spotted last year in front of Big Daddy's eating a hamburger.

Then along came Goldie, a boardwalk troll, pulling a little red wagon behind her. She begged change from everyone, but if anyone gave her coins, she'd throw them back in their face yelling, "Cheapskate!" She preferred bills.

I'd seen her earlier on the basketball courts, racing across the blacktop so fast her wagon was up on two wheels, shoving as much stuff into it as it would fit— mittens, teddy bears, manicure sets, toothbrushes, mini shampoos. "It's for my cousin, it's for my cousin," she kept saying, although no one had asked.

Now Goldie circled Heaven's Pennies. As I stirred the soup, she shoved a packet of string beans and a bag of radishes into the corner of her wagon.

One of Goldie's friends came along next, a person so old and buried in cardigans they'd been relieved of a gender. "Come to Henry's and go halves on smokes?" They opened up their hands like dirty napkins to reveal a palmful of quarters.

Goldie eyed her heavy wagon and then eyed me. "I'll leave this here," she said loudly and indicated her wagon with her toe. "Just leave this here a minute."

The late afternoon sun came out, glancing off storefront windows, orange dapples of light coming down like fat coins tossed from the sky. The warmth of Los Angeles in my bones like good medicine. Heaven's Pennies felt peaceful for a minute.

Lisa sidled over to me. "That Goldie's wagon? She got a good haul this year. She got to have at least ten, twelve pairs of mittens in that thing."

As I stirred the soup, throwing in snap peas and radishes, oatmeal, paprika, I saw the family coming over. The family had been dragged into manning Tony's table so often that at first, I'd thought it was their operation.

Lisa said they came from Ethiopia, a father, a mom, and four little ones, the fourth a baby in its mother's arms. They didn't have a stroller. If they had shelter it was barely. They were out on the boardwalk at sun-up, clothes slept-in, faces unwashed. The tops of the children's black hair had been burned orange-gold from the sun, and they dressed in old tuxedos and cast-off skirts, hems dragging along the cement.

"Hey, Lisa," the mom said, baby hanging from her arms like an iguana. "Hey, girl," she said to me. She held on to her baby with one hand and adjusted her wig with the other. Her red lipstick was all over the place, and one of her eyes kept creeping off. Her lanky husband hung his head—he only had two expressions: bewilderment and disappointment.

"Your family get enough for the holiday? You go by the basketball courts near Muscle Beach?" Lisa dished them up five cups of soup. I began filling a plastic bucket with water from one of the boardwalk spigots for the next batch.

"Time we got there, it's all gone," the mom said, spoon-feeding her baby some ramen broth. "Hard to get going in the morning sometimes, you know how it is."

I could see Lisa out of the corner of my eye, glancing back and forth up the boardwalk. "No need," she said under her breath. "No need. No need of a woman having ten pairs of kids' mittens." Lisa scanned the boardwalk again, and then went right over to Goldie's wagon and began unpacking it, layer by layer. She handed things out to the little family. "You all want some colouring books? You want some balloons? How about some cake icing?"

The children held up the hems of their polyester costumes with one hand and accepted mittens and crayons with the other. They passed the gifts around to each other, admiring their new belongings with coin-bright eyes.

Lisa came and stood beside me, took the spoon out of my hands and stirred the soup, splashing it up the sides of the pot. She steadied her breath, nodded to herself. "Mhm," I heard her say.

But Goldie was back. "What happened to my stuff? Who looted my wagon!" She stood in the middle of the boardwalk and screeched, a long, crazy chicken sound. Her hands on her hips, the wind blowing her white-orange hair out nightmarishly. Tourists gave her a wide berth. Local hippies, used to witnessing a spectacle, ignored her.

Lisa fixed Goldie with a cold hard expression. Anyone less crazy would have taken this as a cue to leave, but Goldie stood her ground, pulling her hair in outrage. She tried to spit on the boardwalk, but the gob landed on her own shoe. The family shuffled off discreetly.

Lisa wagged the soup spoon at Goldie. "You don't get to have all the mittens in Los Angeles," she told her. "You take what you need, and you share the rest. Merry Christmas."

Goldie stood there for a minute, shocked and flapping her mouth, and then ran at the table. I flinched and backed up.

"God will judge you!" She grabbed the edge of the table, shaking it. Cartons of cherry tomatoes and packets of ramen scattered across the concrete. "Thieves! Thieves!" she howled at the passing tourists. "There are thieves in your midst!" No one did anything. Everyone came down to the boardwalk for the drama; there was always a scene. Goldie wouldn't quit. She began pacing back and forth in front of the table, her voice sawing the air. "Jesus judges! Jesus saw what happened. You're going to go to hell!"

Lisa began stirring the soup methodically, her knuckles whitening on the handle. I stood behind her, the folding table giving me a false sense of security. "Everybody deals with Christmas in their own way," she muttered.

Goldie finally acted as if she were about to walk away, but I made the mistake of meeting her eye. She flew back at me. "You," she panted, the rancid fumes of her breath coming out in waves. "You might be saved. Give me my things and you might find mercy! But if you don't, the Lord will curse you. Think about this. Think hard." She raised her veiny purpled fist into the air and shook it desperately.

"All right, enough is enough!" Lisa slammed her hand down on the table. "You have two seconds to get away from this table, or I'll get 6-Up over here so fast it will make your head spin. You share on Christmas. You can go back to being a fool tomorrow." She started toward Goldie, who finally had the sense to flee. I decided not to volunteer at Heaven's Pennies again.

A few weeks later the LAPD shut down Tony's table. Rumours circulated. He'd been using Heaven's Pennies as a front for drugs. Or there'd been food poisonings. Others said he didn't have a licence, some bureaucracy he hadn't paid attention to. But people still hovered around as if Tony might show up once more, unfold his table and offer them food.

Good Luck Friends

The curator of the gallery on Abbot Kinney distributed 3-D glasses in a basket with one hand and clutched a glass of white wine in the other.

One of the paintings showed a flaming abandoned city, hulking shards of molten metal crumbling from an apocalyptic orange sky, a horizon of apartment buildings turning to ashen snow. Trickles of blackened people wearing their belongings on their backs crossed over into a verdant other world, trees and freedom and blue skies, dancing in the 3-D glasses.

The other painting showed a well-fed white couple roaring over a road in a glittering city, dollar bills raining from a sky lit with neon. They tossed a hamburger from their red convertible, one bite taken. The hamburger divided the painting down the middle, and on the other side of the work was a shambles of a village with an unpaved path. Emaciated people clamoured in a pile for the cast-off food, their faces pulled tight in despair and starvation.

Half-Peach and I were the only ones in the gallery who had walked in off the beach. Everyone else had their cars parked by a valet. We left our backpacks on a bench in the entranceway. The elements of the room, silk and wine and security, easy laughter, strategic conversation, shifted around me—I stood in front of a painting, 3-D glasses sliding down my nose. Over the tops of the frames I watched Half-Peach wandering through the gallery, their straw hat bobbing above the heads of strangers.

"Hi, hello, miss. Miss."

I almost knocked the wine from her delicate hand, a hand with golden skin, perfectly pink fingernails. Her eyes widened in a second of panic, but she smoothed herself again. "Miss," she said, clearing her throat. "Are those your ... bags? Piled up? All over our bench right there?" Her graceful finger pointed out our packs, the tin cups hanging off the sides, the rolled sleeping bags snapped to the bottom. Through her eyes, my bag was not proof of my ability to survive but evidence of what was wrong with me.

Half-Peach came tiptoeing over. "Everything okay?" they whispered to me.

"No, everything is *not* okay," said the woman. Her eyes were the exact colour of pewter. "Are those your bags?" She said it slowly, loudly, as if she didn't expect Half-Peach to understand her.

I removed my 3-D glasses—they seemed foolish now. "Yes," I answered, as loudly and slowly as her. "Those are our bags."

People looked over at Half-Peach and me, whispering. There was a security guard at the door, dressed in a blue suit. He watched. The woman extracted a cellphone from her pocket. "You're making our gallery look like a pigpen."

"That's a little rude," I said, but it was a losing battle and Half-Peach and I already knew it.

"If I'm rude then I'm rude." She shrugged and turned to the man by the door, snapped her fingers to summon him. He smelled of pine and whiskey. "Have you noticed how these street people all have the exact same chip on their shoulder?" She laughed with him and lazily held up her phone. "I'm calling the cops."

But we knew to leave before that.

Time was the only thing I was rich with, but too much of it could become a problem. It was easy to lose track of the days. One had to lay low, stay safe, make money, eat, sleep, wash. And manage all of this without getting arrested. Time did not feel linear but circular. There was no forward, there was only round and round and round.

Trash-picking in Venice Beach became a way to pass the hours. The alleys were busy with castoffs and scavengers. Professional pickers drove up and down in flatbed trucks, hauling away furniture the rich had tired of. The bums only looked out for bottles and cans, rattling over the broken pavement with shopping carts and plastic bags, fingers curled like claws.

I learned the back side of every store along Abbot Kinney. Though I didn't really need anything, I liked walking through the alleys in the morning because it was peaceful. I could have been anywhere, in any city. When I came across bottles and cans, I passed them along to the old men and they got to know me that way.

Once I found an old leather motorcycle jacket. Maybe it had belonged to Peter Fonda or Willie Nelson. It was covered in mildew. I went to the CVS to spray it with mould remover. When the drugstore employee told me to get lost, I abandoned the jacket on the sidewalk. Everything came easily and left as fast. Shit just slipped through my fingers—Chinese lanterns, bouquets of wrinkled flowers, old dresses, cloth-bound books, silk pajamas. I wore things and held things and let them go again.

Around this time, Tammy came to town. Tammy carried around a ten-foot-long didgeridoo she had turned into a bong. She wore a filmy flowered curtain like a cape over a neon blue bodysuit and boots with curly toes. She had short, shiny candy-pink hair and silver braces sparkling in the sun. She must have been cared for once, with orthodontic work like that. But she wound up on the boardwalk all the same.

The kids on the boardwalk had to be creative, outsmarting police and outdoing the buskers. The first time I saw her, she was sitting cross-legged on the boardwalk, alternately smoking from her didgeridoo bong and shouting at the tourists, "Magic spells, twenty-five cents! I'll cast a spell for a quarter!" I sat beside her for a while and a photographer came over and took our picture for a magazine. Everyone got their fifteen minutes in Los Angeles.

A powerfully built kid named Gummy Bear introduced himself to Tammy and me as we sat. He wore sunglasses with *Dose* on one lens and *Me* on the other. That's how they all described doing acid: getting dosed. Gummy Bear set up a trading blanket beside us and began putting out incredible trinkets: bone china teacups, leather books.

"I see you seeing," Gummy Bear called over to me.

"You want to trade?" I asked him.

"I don't know ..." he said doubtfully. "It's gotta be quality goods."

I ran into the alleyway and found the red dumpster belonging to the surf and skate shop. They usually threw away the best things. I flung wide the heavy lid and peeked inside. I found a crumpled pile of cast-off backpacks, damaged T-shirts. There was a scattered handful of pens, a valuable commodity, and finally three pairs of barely ruined jeans.

I traded it all for a curlicued skeleton key and a tiny leather-bound bible with a four-leaf clover pressed into page 420. When Gummy Bear asked me if I wanted to get a hotel room with him, I said no thank you.

Another girl I met on the boardwalk was Jules. She was like a cartoon character, the way she only wore one set of clothes—a butcher's apron covered in oil paint, shredded jeans, paint-streaked blond hair, black gloves with the fingers cut off. She smelled of turpentine and unfiltered cigarettes. Her eyeliner smudged in the hollows under her eyes. She flew back and forth between Brooklyn and her studio off Abbot Kinney, a converted garage that was anonymous until she pointed it out.

Jules painted vivid murals of daisies and exaggerated palm trees into the bricks of cafés and the sides of bread trucks. When I met her for the first time in front of Abbot's Habit, it was because her dog came running over to meet Little Wing, the small animals shaking like wire sculptures in the wind.

"Sloppy Joe, come on, man." And there was Jules, a painter notorious for the murals she did all over the neighbourhood. She was famous in the way the man in the American flag speedo and rollerblades was famous, a fixture of life on the boardwalk.

I bent over to pat the chihuahua named Sloppy Joe, but he bared his tiny teeth at me.

"Better not touch him. Sloppy Joe is a real train wreck. He'll lock onto one of your fingers and won't let go." Jules tucked him under her arm like a parcel. Sloppy Joe scowled at me. "You might need those fingers. I've seen you playing guitar."

"Oh. Sometimes I play, just as a way to make a little change. I've never noticed you."

"Then it's working," she said and tucked Sloppy Joe more securely beneath her arm. He issued a snarling protest and quieted again. Little Wing, who was more respectable, sat silently on the end of my shoe.

"What's working?"

"Invisibility. Being a girl is a dangerous trade. Why are you going around here all flashy and sticking out? Doesn't it make you nervous?"

I looked down at my clothes, seeing them with new eyes. I hadn't thought of myself as flashy. I wore whatever I found—flowered blouses, plaid pants. I wore them until I was bored and then left them wherever I found something new.

"It's 'cause you always got some boy around you," said Jules. "But they're the ones you gotta watch out for the most."

I wondered what she'd heard about me then. I wondered if there were stories about me going around the streets, just like the stories I heard about other drifters and locals.

Jules took me to her studio, the secret place from which her paintings sprung forth fully formed. She pulled up the garage door with a rattling clatter—it only went up halfway—and we ducked into the darkness. A bare hanging bulb lit the studio up: stacks of canvas, rickety easels crowded into the corners, a broken-down couch. A mattress on the floor piled with blankets and, barely visible, a few fuzzy sleeping heads. They groaned in the light and pulled the blankets over their faces.

"I'm working on a new series," Jules said, pointing out a couple of canvases leaning on the far wall. "It's called Naked Neighbours."

I recognized shop owners and café regulars, flat and shining from the canvases propped against her studio wall, paint thick as frosting, naked parts revealed like the inner workings of a clock.

"You should let me paint you having sex with Leo," said Jules. "You make an attractive couple." She let Sloppy Joe down onto the concrete floor and he scurried beneath the couch, shitting rabbit-pellet turds along the way.

"I'm through with all that." I remembered what Jules said about the boys I kept around. I wanted her to change her mind about me.

Jules shrugged and began rolling a joint. Heat blazed in through the half-open garage doorway, the morning full on. She put on a pair of plastic heart-shaped sunglasses and we went back outside, sitting against the stucco garage wall on warm cement. From beyond the quiet street came the washing drone of freeway traffic. Jules looking me over with her artist's eye—I could feel her analysis. As it turned tense, Vegas came running up the sidewalk.

Vegas was Jules's best friend. They'd grown up together in Santa Monica. She worked in a dress shop on Abbot Kinney. She had a face round as the moon. Jules had painted a portrait of Vegas, topless with her tongue out, her tiny hands covering her nipples. *High School Graduate* scribbled across her chest in black marker.

Vegas came to gossip. She sprawled easily beside Jules, snatching the joint and puffing on it, grabbing Sloppy Joe and holding him to her face. The dog licked her nose with affection.

"Genevieve is killing me, she's the most pathetic wannabe," Vegas told Jules, stretching out her toned, tanned legs. She blew a smoke ring, tossed her hair. Genevieve, Jules told me, was the dress shop owner. "If she gets any more fillers, her face is going to burst. She looks like a blowfish with hot dog lips." Genevieve had opened the dress shop with her father's money. It was an orgy of velvet and paisley and feathers—old Los Angeles psychedelia with the sterility of contemporary gentrification. In the days that followed, I would go there with Jules and sit on the fat floor pillows, stoned, running my hands along the hems of dresses that cost so much I couldn't even make sense of the numbers.

"Come on, Jules, let's drive into Laurel Canyon and look at Joni Mitchell's house." Vegas said this to Jules, but she was looking at me because she didn't want me to come. I hadn't grown up with these girls or shared their secrets. Vegas took hold of Jules's fingers and licked her like a cat, intimacies that didn't belong to me.

"Hey sir, you hungry? We found this bag on the sidewalk. There's some evaporated milk and a can of chicken soup." Half-Peach and I spent the afternoon playing guitar on the boardwalk and made enough for burgers at Big Daddy's. I liked to eat on the warm blacktop under the seagulls, sky shining white with winter sun, cars roaring around us, my salty fingers, the lurid blue facade of Big Daddy's held up by white columns like a castle under the sea.

We kept winding up together, Half-Peach and I, both of us shy and rootless. They brought out a flowery, gentle side of me. I could be less tough around them. It had been getting harder and harder to be soft, to think beyond the boardwalk, beyond Los Angeles. But Half-Peach felt familiar as my own self.

The old man limped over, his blue eyes light as ice, his cheekbones skeletal. He smiled. "Thank you for that. Thanks to you." He took the plastic grocery bag from Half-Peach. "My name's Sark. I'm from Germany." His voice lilted with proof.

"How'd you wind up in Los Angeles?" I asked him. I liked hearing people's origin stories.

"Got kidnapped when I was a boy. They hit me over the head with a stone. I woke up on a ship. Life comes at you in sections. The only part I understand is the part I'm in. Actually, I don't know about understand. None of this makes sense. But I am an alchemist. I will figure it out." The sun came down on his white hair and on the pink skin beneath; it lit him up in beams as if this too were alchemy. He began digging around in the pocket of his jeans and extracted a rough chunk of crystal glass, jagged and faceted, blinking in the light. He held the glass up to his eye and looked through it at the world. Then he put it in the palm of my hand. "This will protect you."

Out and About

Little boys sold broken bracelets, out-of-season Santa hats and cracked chocolate bars all along the boardwalk, running through the streets, too young to be so stoned. They ran up to the celebrities sitting at outdoor restaurants and held out their hands. They tore up and down the sand in packs.

One night, a diabetic man got drunk with a bunch of others on the boardwalk. When his organs failed, they wrapped him in a blanket and left him on a bench, his head lolling, his hand grazing the ground. When the paramedics came, they loaded him onto the stretcher slowly and covered his face with a sheet. Behind the scene of flashing lights was the smell of diesel and salt, the indigo sky laced with smoke from fires on the beach.

An old man had been biking down the boardwalk, high out of his mind, when he flipped and ripped his face open on the concrete. You could see inside his eyebrow down to the bone, the gash so deep it didn't bleed. A woman came by with a sewing kit and stitched his face with a fabric needle while he sat there laughing and stretching his arms above his head.

There was a boy on the boardwalk who everyone called Pirate because of the polyester pirate Halloween costume he wore. He often brandished a plastic sword at tourists and screamed "Argh" in their faces. But one day he showed up on the boardwalk pacing and moaning, finally pulling down his pants to show a big oozing abscess leaking milky pus down the side of his leg.

Pirate's friend was stabbed in the face for enraging the Bloods. A whole mess of them came down to the boardwalk, lurid in red. There was a confrontation—they made it look like a shoving match, but the boy got a knife to the cheek that almost split his mouth. The Bloods dispersed amongst the tourists while sirens sawed along the edge of the horizon. It was Puck who first was on the scene, coming out from under his big orange beach umbrella carrying a first aid kit. I watched him nimbly dress the wound.

Puck and Brian were old friends. They biked all over Venice Beach with their black cat, Shiva, in a basket, their bikes heavy with beach balls and radios and wooden walking sticks that Puck carved and sold on the boardwalk during the afternoons. When they weren't biking, they sat under the orange umbrella. Brian had been a surfer in the seventies and still had the lean, lanky body. His long blond hair and sun-wrinkled face marked him as a local straight away. Puck said he was from New York. He spiked his hair straight up, wore silver jewellery and chain-smoked cigarettes. In the evening, they played frisbee and put out towels like common tourists, as if they had nowhere else to be in the world.

It was New Year's Eve and there'd been a big party on the beach, everything lit up and fiery. The holiday made me feel safe enough to wander around alone. New Year's Eve was for everyone: the fireworks, the brand new year with no mistakes yet in it.

I headed to my sleeping spot in the first hours of the new year. I was sleeping in the library parking lot again. The neighbourhood seemed full of light, the roar of the ongoing party coming from the water's edge. I cut through the side streets, feeling good, when I came across Puck curled up under an awning. Brian was not with him, which was unusual. Puck looked sick. He was sweaty and grey in the face.

"Puck?" I crouched down beside him. "Are you all right?"

Puck forced a tight grin. "Yes, yes, sure. I saw a psychic tonight, that's all."

"Oh?"

He was having a panic attack. Puck pulled his sleeping bag tighter around him. "She said I'm gonna die. She actually said the world is coming to an end." He tried to catch his breath. I didn't know what to do; he was only a man I saw around town. "She said the seas are going to rise up and swallow us." He wiped the back of his hand across his forehead.

"Hey, come on now," I said. The night around us seemed quieter now, as if all the parties had stopped. "That woman was a charlatan."

"Then why am I afraid?"

Chief biked around the boardwalk shouting blessings, streaming feathers through the air. He danced himself dizzy in the heart of the drum circle, chanting prayers. He said he wrote a bestselling book. When the police came after him, as the police came after everyone visible on the boardwalk, he claimed sanctuary on the beach because he said that's what it was.

In the parking lot at night, he biked up to me and introduced himself. "If someone hassles you, you come tell me," he said. He showed me a silver sheriff-style badge pinned to the front of his jacket that said *Universe Protector*.

He told me warning stories about the kid who got caught selling fake drugs to the Bloods. The boy turned up on the beach buried to the neck. His whole body had been cut open, hollowed out and filled with sand. "But don't worry about the troublemakers," he said. "You know how we handle troublemakers down here? Don't go to LAPD, they're trouble too, you watch out for them. We handle our own. Here in Venice we run 'em off the beach, ocean direction. Or else we have a sand party. Dig a hole, stick 'em in it, and make 'em wait for the tide. Don't tell anyone where you're from. Don't tell anyone your name or anything about you. Take on a nickname, pick a place, think up a story and tell someone. They'll pass it around for you. The truth don't exist. The truth is a weapon pressed to your throat at night."

The drifters rarely went onto the beach proper because you couldn't smoke and dogs weren't allowed unless you were famous. The beach was too vast and pure, too natural for LA. Trash pickers, tweakers and swindlers couldn't scam the sea. It could swallow you and it would be like you never were.

But that day we were restless. Jay, Alex, Half-Peach, Twist and I traipsed out toward the horizon, spread out a tarp and lay on it while the piss-yellow SUVs belonging to the beach police passed us by.

No one owned a bathing suit, and we all went into the stingingly cold water half-clothed. Jay wore a boy's translucent white tank top. As soon as she hit the water, her dark nipples showed through. Alex had a big scar worming down the front of his skinny torso; he said he'd been born with his intestines on the outside of his body.

Someone scraped together a contraband cigarette with a little pocket tobacco, and we passed it around damply with wrinkled fingers.

The night fell subtly all around us, the temperature staying the same. Twist wanted to show everyone his new sleeping spot, so we put together some change for a couple cans of Four Loko and followed him down to the end of the boardwalk, past the parking lot of painted school buses and camper vans, sculptures leaning crazily from the roofs of the vehicles, murals splotchy with stars and tinsel.

Twist's spot was a secluded patch of concrete wall. Down on the cold sand, he showed us a crawl space where he slept. Someone was already under there in a sleeping bag, but we never found out who it was. Twist said it was some old home bum, so we let him be.

He spread out the tarp in the warped winter night and we sat in a circle passing around the cans of cheap candy-coloured booze. Someone started talking about sex and by the time the Four Lokos kicked in, everyone was kissing and groping each other. "Where's Half-Peach's head?" someone asked. "Down there," someone said back. Jay on her knees. Her mouth.

The old home bum under the concrete wall never stirred.

Afterward, slowly puffing on hand-rolled cigarettes, Nicki came running along the wall up above. She was a loud-mouthed runaway who looked nineteen but was much younger and was constantly taken advantage of because of it. She had been sleeping in the same parking garage as Twist, but her silly troubles had driven him to this new spot.

"Heard you all were having some kind of orgy!" Nicki shouted obnoxiously. She was puffing on a fat cigar butt, proudly picking fresh tweaker scabs.

"Nicki, go home to your mom and dad!" Twist yelled, pulling his coat around him.

She stuck out her tongue and wandered off.

There was acid going around. Jay and Alex spent a night high on the boardwalk telling everyone there would be a tsunami because they felt it. The next day, it turned out there had been a minor tsunami in Malibu. After that everyone wanted a hit.

Half-Peach, Kriel and I were loitering around Big Daddy's one evening when a big, swaying drunk came up to us. His name was Chuck, and he bought us all hamburgers without being asked. He was friendly like a bear, shouting his words. We ate in the parking lot on the warm hood of a stranger's car, licking salt from our fingers. Chuck wanted to go to the liquor store. Half-Peach, Kriel and I followed him over there, waiting outside while he strolled the fluorescent store as confidently as if it were his own house. He selected a bottle as big as my arm.

We went leisurely through the streets with the man. He talked easily about how he used to live on the boardwalk like us. The world was too expensive, and we needed to share our money with each other. But what did I need with money? Nothing had cost me anything yet.

We sprawled out under the fig tree by the dog park, vodka-drunk. Tonight I was comfortable. I was full. I knew the streets, I had my friends, and wasn't that the feeling of home? Full stomach and a place to sit? Usually I felt like a squirrelly ragamuffin, ashamed and defiant in it. All of that was washed clean in vodka. I was baptized in the stinging waters. I felt bold and tough, merry and beautiful.

When the vodka got low, Alex and Jay came stumbling along as if they'd been cued by our dwindling supplies. They had the good LSD.

The tree made a living room, bark walls and hanging branch roof, constellation animals dancing across the screen of the loose, zany dark. Our nonsense talk scribbled on the sky.

Chuck bellowed like a madman. His words were so foolish I wiped my crying eyes, I didn't even know what he was saying. Kriel held her ribs, both of us leaning on one another, shaking with hysteria. Alex had a guitar in his lap, twanging at it tunelessly and holding up the instrument in awe to watch the strings vibrate with sound. "String theory," he said. "String theory!" He jumped to his feet and then sat back down again, stunned. Anytime anyone said something profound, the fig tree dropped a knuckling of hard fruit on our heads.

Deep in the night an unknown man came over to our tree and, without saying anything, fell asleep on the other side of the trunk. "It's the dude on the couch," said Alex. I went over and put a blanket on him. He didn't move.

When we ran out of cigarettes, Half-Peach, Kriel and I volunteered to go out into the neighbourhood to find a convenience store. I stood shakily, my knees full of air, and walked an inch above the concrete. It seemed like it took a very long time to find the store. The mission was epic, navigating the wide and twisting streets lined with palm trees and protective fences.

The canyons were heavy with expensive structures, the city patched up as a crazy quilt. I bobbed through the dark folds, completely anonymous. No one even knew I was here, right where I was.

The deep hills had been full of musicians, a future anyone could have grabbed. But those ideas were so shiny and idiotic; did anyone really once believe sunshine would save you? Dahlia, the jewellery maker, lived with seven other people and three dogs in a one-bedroom apartment. Where was their pie in the sky? It was more of a circle game than those flowered airheads could have ever conceived.

Who had been in the megalopolis when it had only been dirt and sky? Who was in the canyons first? Who had fished the waters and browned in the sun for free?

As we walked along to buy smokes at the store, I trailed my fingers across the white wooden slats of picket fences and over the prickly hedges that penned in perfect beach homes.

Drifting easily from the open windows came the sounds of glasses clinking, a jazz horn, a sleepy piano. People danced lazily across their million-dollar living rooms. A film of curtain pulled across a yellow pane. They wanted to be seen. I saw. I did what they wanted me to do: I longed. I wanted to sink my teeth into their lives.

Someone dropped a wine glass on the hardwood. I held the spikes of their wrought iron fence, letting my friends who were only with me by chance walk ahead. I held the cold bars and I knew this could be my entire life, this longing and looking in. There was the tinkling shush of the shards being swept. I let go of the fence and caught up to my friends, and we went into the store, fluorescent lights hard and cold against the night.

When we got back to the tree, Alex cackled that the Dude on the Couch had woken up, and he'd dosed him. Sure enough, the Dude on the Couch was up and laughing like a bandit.

Then it was six in the morning and Alex and Jay were buried in a sleeping bag and the Dude on the Couch staggered off to find his car.

It was Half-Peach who suggested we go to the beach. The seediness of dawn made me feel too big for my skin. I could see the rest of their faces, uneasy in the coming of another day—none of us different than before, even though there should have been miracles.

Alex and Jay stayed behind in the sleeping bag, so it was only Half-Peach, Kriel, Chuck and me, as it had been when the night began. When we reached the cold sand, Kriel went to the ruffling lip of the ocean and stood there alone, dancing. Chuck was white in the face and muttered something about going to find coffee, but he never came back. Before he left, he handed Half-Peach the rest of the acid, wrapped in tinfoil.

Half-Peach and I went up onto the deck of one of the lifeguard huts, ducking from the slap of the wind. The crests of waves looked like restless reaching hands being pulled back down by the black ocean. The sky was grubby in the dawn, the rush of water a swishing froth between my ears.

"Do this with me?" Half-Peach held out a little scrap of acid on their fingertip. But then they put it in their own mouth and pulled me close, transferring the acid with their tongue.

Kriel and I slumped at the tables in front of the coffee shop, slack-jawed and fried. The hot old morning groaned along and dragged us with it.

Debbie-Cathy, one of the old home bum women notorious for causing a commotion, came tottering over, her wiry hair electrified. Debbie-Cathy wore miniskirts with no underwear, harassed any man she could find and was always fucked up on something by nine in the morning.

"Black cock is superior," she screamed at us by way of greeting. "I'm going to Compton to steal some children on the train! They'll come get me and BAM! That's how I'll do it." She did a little dance to accompany her plan.

Kriel put her face into her hands, shaking. I cried behind my sunglasses.

"Y'all aren't laughing at me, are you?" Debbie-Cathy hollered. She jerked her head wildly, as overstimulated as I felt.

Kriel wiped her eyes. "We did acid last night."

"Oh." Debbie-Cathy nodded sagely. "All right then." And wandered off.

When the rains came, Half-Peach left again for Humboldt County, something about visiting an old friend. I said good-bye outside Big Daddy's, the blue paint of the place garish in the gloom. Half-Peach was a self-described Travelling Kid. They said they would pass through Venice Beach again depending on whether they could get a crew change guide, the holy document that kept train-hoppers from winding up in Milwaukee when they were trying to get to New York.

"Come find me," they said. But they were already fussing with their backpack, thoughts on other things.

It was spring, and cold. I had been taking shelter in the Santa Monica library when I met Nate. A big farm boy, he slouched over a public computer, crying the shaking, silent tears of crisis. I noticed the camping backpack at his feet and figured he was in the same position as me, socioeconomically speaking.

He'd been in California barely two weeks from Iowa, he told me. He came out of boredom and curiosity. But then his father died after he left, and nobody had been able to reach him until today. Nate was out of money and wanted to go home but couldn't afford it. Not only was his father dead, but he would miss the funeral. He was helpless with grief and didn't know where to sleep. He was going to try and find a homeless shelter, but I told him he could come with me.

Because of the rain, I'd been asking around for dry spots to camp, but they were highly coveted and hardly available. I remembered Twist had moved on from his place at the parking garage, so that night Nate and I went to suss it out. Along the way, we bought a bottle of whiskey to have a wake for his father.

The parking garage was eerily empty on the damp and rainy night. I had expected it to be crowded with people from the street.

"Looks like we have our pick," I said to Nate, trying to sound cheerful. He only shrugged and took a slug of whiskey. He didn't have a sleeping bag. I offered to unzip mine and spread it out. Our footsteps echoed as we walked, our voices bouncing off the walls. The smell of oil-stained cement.

In a corner, two scrawny teenagers slept in their own spots as if they were vehicles come to park, laid up with raggedy blankets and sleeping bags, a portable radio going full blast, the Doors or some other Los Angeles fluff. Nate and I asked if we could camp out next to them. It was safer to sleep next to other people than away from them—that way they couldn't sneak up on you in the night and, if they had no plans to rob you, you'd be safe with numbers.

The teenagers were strung out and fucked up, though. "Yeah, yeah," they said, shaking and cross-eyed. Nate looked at me, nervous as a puppy. "It's fine," I mouthed to him before unrolling my sleeping bag and laying it out.

Now I knew why the parking garage was empty at night. The blinding floodlights lining the ceiling stayed on all night. Sleeping on damp concrete made your bones ache after just a few minutes, and so Nate and I sat with our backs to the wall, our legs stretched out in front of us, passing the bottle back and forth. Sometimes there was a weird shrieking noise coming from the levels below, a rattling, echoing holler as some troublemakers came and went. Still somehow my head became heavy and I drifted away.

What woke me was a man in a trench coat. His shadow fell across my face and blocked out the floodlights so the darkness made me open my eyes. Immediately a pounding headache gripped my skull.

Beside me, Nate snored like a bear, his chin on his chest. The teenagers had been waiting for this man. They sat up, suddenly all business, and began rifling through their bags, pulling out loose bills. The man waited until he was sure they'd brought out all they had, and then he made a big production of saying, "All right, but this is the last time. After this, I'm not coming around no more." He dug around in his deep pockets, taking his time, pretending he might not find what they wanted. The man had a hood pulled low on his head and a bandana tied over the lower half of his face.

It had to be four in the morning at least. I sat there not moving. If I kept very still, the man would go away again, and I would be fine. While he fished around for the tin-foil packets, the teenagers began preparing their needles. Not wanting to miss out on any possible hustle, he turned to me.

"It's China White. These two knuckleheads get discounts 'cause this is the spot I come at night. Since you're sleeping here, I'll give you the same deal. If you ain't got no cash, we can work somethin' out, always a way." And he grabbed the front of his pants to show me what way he meant.

"I'm fine," I said.

But even after his clients nodded back to sleep, he continued to hover, blocking out the light. Waiting to see if I'd surrender to his sales pitch. His eyes glistening, darting. The night was still as oil around us. There was only him and me. The only ones awake in the world. Watching me, he leaned against the wall. He waited for me to close my eyes. I didn't.

I slowly moved my hand, making it look like I was only stretching, and jogged Nate's arm. The man saw everything and only watched to see what Nate would do. Nate did not say anything. He looked at me. I looked at him. The man in the trench coat hesitated and slowly peeled himself away from the wall, strutting off. His foot-steps echoed throughout the parking garage long after he was out of sight. Nate and I sat there, just like that, until the sun was in the sky.

Twist had a new sleeping spot at Heartbreak Hotel, but he said he'd have to bring me in. I couldn't show up there alone. Heartbreak Hotel was an abandoned half-constructed condominium project, some rich developer's hobby that fizzled out. Everyone said the wiring had been done badly and it would have taken even more money to tear it down and start over. The yuppies pretended it didn't exist, which meant we could have it for ourselves.

To get in, you had to pull back a heavy piece of chain-link fence and then crawl down a dirt incline into the belly of the building, an empty parking garage pitch-black even in the afternoon. You had to walk down the middle of the garage, one foot in front of the other in the blackness, to the far wall. Once you got there, a door opened to a set of stairs going up into the apartments. The rooms were big and empty, full of light and warmed by the sun. Stacks of abandoned drywall, the only stuff in the raw-wood rooms, made fine beds. I imagined velvet sofas, lamps with stained glass shades casting coloured light across the walls. Deep carpets, fridges full of food. Running water. Toilets. But we had shelter and that was good enough.

After Twist brought me in, I brought in Nate and Kriel, who brought in little Carolina. The cold rain came down in hard, relentless fistfuls. I had learned to associate rain with trouble.

The longer the rain fell, the more kids piled into Heartbreak Hotel. Twist couldn't stop them. They all knew about the squat. So did the police. They had busted the place once before and thrown whatever they found—sleeping bags, guitars, shoes, clothes—into the dumpsters and covered it with wet cement. I carried my belongings with me everywhere.

The rain didn't stop. Heartbreak Hotel reeked like wet dog, mildew, feet. The corners of the big, open rooms were crowded with tweakers blaring punk rock from their radios at night, too high to care about cops.

After only a few days of bad weather, every unit in the building had been opened, overrun and trashed.

It was exhausting to be always ready to spring, every muscle tensed. I got tired. This was when I was stupid. I'd left my belongings in Heartbreak Hotel one afternoon while walking Little Wing around the block under the watery sky. Other people had been letting their dogs shit in the parking garage and on the stairs, but just because we were homeless didn't mean we had to abandon decorum. The others teased me for carrying a toothbrush, toothpaste and a washcloth. They said I was high maintenance. They used anger to keep from feeling the loss of their human rights. But I needed my rituals. Anything else felt like giving up.

When I came back, Little Wing and I waded through the darkness of the parking garage, the tiny click of her nails on the concrete. But when I found the stairwell door, it was locked. I rapped my knuckles on the wood. "Hello?"

Someone inside screamed, "Get the fuck outta here!"

I knocked louder. There was the sound of someone storming down the stairs. I braced myself.

A gentle touch on my shoulder from behind. I whipped around to see Twist. "What's going on?" he asked.

"Door's locked."

When Twist knocked, the door got opened. The person who opened it, a brawny teenager, fled back up the stairs. Twist shrugged. "Let's go see what's going on," he said, and I followed him inside.

The apartment that Twist, Kriel, Nate, Carolina and I had claimed was completely destroyed. I knew it had been getting bad, but I rarely saw the place in the daylight. Now the place was flooded with afternoon sun. I saw everything. Garbage strewn all over the floor, beer bottles, cigarette butts, piles of human shit, mildewed clothes. Putrid socks hung up on the wooden beams to dry. The smell was unbelievable.

A gang guarded the place; they'd been sleeping in another part of the squat, but now it seemed like they were trying to take over while we were gone. Their wardrobes were busy with gold chains and red bandanas. I tried to push past them, and they rose up against me like a human wave, as if to wash me back down the stairs. But Twist stood behind me, and I was protected with him there. Most of the gang members were so stoned they could barely open their eyes anyway. A smoke came from them, the sweet smell of burning plastic drugs. Twist shuffled them out of my way so I could gather my things, and as I left, I could hear him roaring.

I collided with Jay and Alex once I reached the street. They jauntily swung a bag of wine and were looking for trouble. When I told them about the scene inside Heart-break Hotel, they ran off eagerly to join the fray. I headed back to the beach alone.

The Rose Den

The smell of black mould and rotten wood permeated the room, a sweet decay. After a few days of relentless fever, I probably should have been in the hospital, but I was Canadian so I had to sweat it out.

The Rose Den was once white, but the paint had slowly peeled away to reveal ocean-soft wood beneath. The yard was buried beneath Jurassic palm bushes and shrubs. The living room was crowded with bookshelves and cardboard boxes, a wheelbarrow missing its wheel, two rusty clawfoot bathtubs. There was one bedroom, its lone window looking out on an overgrown backyard. The room was empty except for a mattress on an iron frame and a closet alive with the sounds of spiders. You got into the cottage by crawling through the fence, wading through the long grass and pushing in the back door that led directly into that bedroom.

It was still raining. The hitchhikers and travellers and local drifters were competing for shelter, so Alex was very strict about who was allowed into the Rose Den. "I'm not having another scene like the one at Heartbreak," he told me. "Next thing you know, this place will be full of junkies and gangs and cops." He let me into the cottage on the condition I came alone.

The gangs and cops were a legitimate worry in Venice Beach. I'd seen the gangs rolling along the boardwalk, scattering rivals with the wave of a weapon. I kept the warning stories I'd heard at the front of my head to stay sharp. The stories of the LAPD were just as bad; they were known for bursting into abandoned buildings and beating and arresting whoever they grabbed. We could exist so long as we kept our existence to ourselves.

It was probably the rain that brought on my fever. I had been out in it, walking around on the boardwalk with ruined shoes and dripping hair. Staying dry had become a challenge.

Alex was the only person I knew in the Rose Den, if you could call our street interactions a knowing. There were three others camping in the cottage besides me: Sketchy, Curly and Boo. They were hard to tell apart with their missing teeth, straggly dreadlocks and flannel shirts. They were friends of Alex's, only passing through. The three of them went out during the day to bum spare change off the tourists on the boardwalk. They called it *sp'anging.* When they had enough money, they headed into Hollywood for drugs. I didn't know much else about them other than where they slept.

Every morning I woke up sick, my entire body on fire, heavy as a bag of rocks. As soon as my eyes opened, my head began to pound. I was so hot that my rain-soaked clothes went from wet to dry and back to wet again. Alex told me I could have the mattress. None of us had been sleeping on it because it wouldn't have been fair for one to have it and not all.

The others milled around the living room, packing up their bags for the day and making plans. When the three boys filed past the bed out the back door they said sweetly, "Feel better." The rain rattled down onto the cottage roof, dampness in the air as thick as mist. Alex stayed behind after the others were gone.

"I'll bring you back some brandy and whatever I can steal from the drugstore," he promised, tugging on his matted hair. "You'll be okay here by yourself?"

"Of course," I said. I was looking forward to the privacy. I was almost never alone. That was for my own safety, but I had forgotten about the richness of a silent day.

Alex found a rag, soaked it in cold water from his canteen and put it on my forehead. Then he went off.

After he was gone, there was only the sound of the rain falling on the roof and dripping down into the corners of the room. My lungs rattled, my skin throbbed. I drifted off and came to again later in the day. The sky was still the same wall of grey. I could hear the traffic of Los

Angeles, its mechanical inhale-exhale. It could have been any hour, any day.

I sat up slowly, pushed my bare feet into my wet shoes and went into the other room. The boys had neatly piled their sleeping things against the far wall.

The ceiling of the room was high, but the tiny windows barely let in any light. The gloom made the cottage feel smaller than it was. I wove between the two rusted bathtubs and went to the bookshelf. Alex called our hideout the Rose Den because of the old man's journals. The journals were not kept in notebooks but instead had been written out on yellow legal pads. There were stacks of them on the shelves; they filled the cardboard boxes; they overflowed onto the floor. I picked one up and began to read.

Two years, six months, twenty days since Rose's passing.

That's how every entry began. He signed each one with, *Thought about Rose all day.* The next entry would read, *Two years, six months, twenty-one days since Rose's passing.*

> Went to the post office this morning and mailed a letter to Marge, who is still in Tampa, even though I have told her to come back. Marge says she's got the cat and the condominium but she has said she will see what she can do.
>
> Went to the drugstore but they did not yet have my pills so was told to come back after two this afternoon.

Came home and made a lunch of boiled eggs and an orange for dessert.

Ran out of clean socks this morning so will do the laundry tomorrow morning.

Thought about Rose all day.

The next day it was raining even harder. No one wanted to go outside; their clothes were still drenched from yesterday. My fever wore heavy on me, but I was bored. The boys and I sat around the bedroom shooting the shit, when Alex came in from the yard, dreadlocks plastered to his face. He said he'd found some porno magazines in the tool shed.

"All right," the boys crowed and went off after Alex. When they opened the bedroom door, the smell of fresh rain came in. I got up slowly, scribbly as an old woman, and walked across the wet grass that soaked my jeans, inhaling the deep smell of earth. I ducked into the corrugated metal shed where the boys crowded. They had a way of taking up all the space, their rough, clumsy bodies swathed in stinking flannel. I pressed in behind them. The shed smelled like soil and wet mould. It was empty except for a few wooden shelves messy with magazines and photographs.

Alex passed me a couple of the photos: black and white ones of a young couple holding hands under a palm tree and sepia ones of a middle-aged couple sitting on a couch opening Christmas presents.

Curly grabbed a porno magazine. "Look at that bush," he whistled. The models had bright blue eyeshadow, red lacquered nails, frosted lipstick, orange tans, and all of them were smiling.

Curly, Sketchy and Boo met a few boys down on the boardwalk and brought them, and their three pit bulls, to the squat that night. Alex found a girl named Sandy who had ridden her bike all the way from New Hampshire and brought her in. The Rose Den was getting crowded.

Two years, seven months, three days since Rose's passing.

Marge came back to Los Angeles and is staying in the neighbourhood. She has been visiting regularly but says I have a degenerative mental illness and that I have to go somewhere where they can give me care.

Leftovers for lunch. The drugstore had my pills this morning.

Thought about Rose all day.

The next night, Boo, Sketchy and Curly came back to the cottage late, drunk with new friends. They came through the bedroom door carrying boxes of beer and a tape player blasting death metal. I was lying on the bed in the dark and they didn't see me. Wild and hollering, they crashed into the living room and stepped on Sandy, who'd been sleeping on the floor. I heard her scream. Somehow a fight broke out. I could hear the thrashing and bellowing, dogs yelping and barking, Sandy shrieking something about her bicycle getting bent. Alex wasn't there. The police would come. The rain hammered violently on the roof. All of this happened in the pitch darkness, although as I peeked around the door frame, I could see a beam of yellow, a lone flashlight slashing through the night. It came from the floor, so it was probably Sandy trying to get away from the punks rolling around the room, throwing punches and boot kicks. In the spastic fray she grabbed her bike and went creaking past me, crying quietly to herself.

I felt for Little Wing, who always had a peaceful sleep no matter where I put her, and grabbed my bag, slipping out into the night. The moonlight was slippery across the grass. The rain came down slow and sleepy and then stopped altogether, a beaded curtain being opened. I stood in the alley breathing the newly washed air, orange street lights gleaming on the pavement.

I wished I could give the cottage a fresh coat of paint and clean out the mildew and spiders. I wished the place wouldn't be torn down and turned into condos or destroyed by drunks who didn't know what they were doing.

I wish I could go back to the little white cottage hidden by palms and see it now, on a sunny Venice Beach morning. The notebooks might even be there still, yellow pages spread across the floor.

Bench Lady

Bench Lady's real name was Maggie. She came from Geor-
gia when she was only fifteen, back in the early seventies.
She loved to scream at people who were behaving badly,
thugs and punks, she had no fear of anyone. She was
beautiful and a drunk. She smoked menthol cigarettes
and fell in love with all the young boys. You could leave
your gear at her bench all day and it was safe because
Maggie didn't move from the time she got up until it was
night, unless she was sashaying down to Henry's Market
to grab more cigarettes. Even then she could usually get
Old John to bike over and get them for her.

Old John was her sweetheart. Salty and crusty, he
came from Liverpool for no better reason than the rest
of us. He took Ecstasy and biked in circles around the
boardwalk, wearing a wool sweater and fisherman's cap.
At night he went with Maggie because everyone needed
someone.

"You have a calming presence," she told me once,
maybe because I didn't say much.

When Maggie first arrived in Los Angeles as a teenager, she'd been kidnapped by a couple of men. They'd grabbed her right off the street and brought her to an old warehouse, raped her over and over, and left her tied up for days. Maggie said she didn't insult them or lose her cool. She didn't cry. She stayed very still and very quiet. Because she knew they would get bored. They were men. She explained that if she'd been afraid, they would have killed her. "That's how you have to be with men, and that's how you have to be around here. They're always watching you. If you're not hurt, it's because they choose not to hurt you."

Behind Maggie's bench was the grass, then the bike path, then the chain-link fence. Then came the sand, the beach, the sea.

We were sprawled in the grass behind Bench Lady's bench, having a lazy afternoon, when I realized I hadn't seen Carolina in a week or so. I asked if anyone else had seen her. They were all quiet: Twist, Jay, Kriel, Alex, Nate. It was Alex who finally spoke up.

"It happened while you were sick in the Rose Den," he said. "I didn't really know how to bring it up ..." He said she'd been staying at a women's shelter but kept getting into trouble for sneaking men through her window, for staying out all night. She was spotted running up and down the boardwalk in all states of undress with any kind of creep. No one was low enough for her. She was mad on acid, grinding her jaw on bad Ecstasy.

In Heartbreak Hotel, Carolina took a handful of mismatched drugs and went from sleeping bag to sleeping bag, offering herself to whoever was there.

In the morning, she was seen weaving among the palm trees like an inner-city Lorelei, wearing a tattered dress, screaming Spanish singsong, reverting to gibberish. She'd gotten ahold of a pair of scissors and in some theatre of the absurd, the crazy boardwalk as her stage, she began hacking off her long gold-black hair. Sawing off sheaves of it, scattering it to the wind. Screaming while she did it. Surrounded by staring strangers.

The police got her in the end. Because she was a minor, they called her mother. The mother reached the boardwalk in five minutes. She had never been far away after all. When she saw her daughter, she fell to her knees. Carolina was tackled by the police. She thrashed and hollered, her hair cut down to her skull. Her mother tried to intercede between her daughter and the LAPD, but they said they were taking her to social services. Carolina only screamed, lost to the inner world of her hallucinations. And finally, beaten into unconsciousness, she was dragged away in the back of a police car and we never saw her again.

"I got myself into some trouble," Kriel told me. "With Noah."

"I remember him," I told her. We sat with our backs to the brick wall of Abbot's Habit, which had a view of the dumpster and the parking lot. It was early enough in the morning that the air was still clean with mist, the streets quiet.

"He was selling drugs." Kriel stared straight ahead at the pavement. "And ripping people off. He'd take their money in the lobby of an apartment and then go upstairs and down the fire escape or something. Chief tipped off everyone on the boardwalk so nobody would go near him anymore. But I was so stupid in love, wanting my babies and husband. Noah assaulted me in the bathrooms on the beach, you know, those flimsy stalls. I went in there and he followed me, said I'd ratted him out 'cause everyone was onto him, and then he's bashing my face in, ripping off my clothes ..." She held her knees against her chest, her arms wrapped around herself, her face blank as the morning. "I'm done with this fucking neighbourhood. I'm going home."

"Where's that?" My sympathy wouldn't undo anything. I was useless beside her.

"North. Paso Robles."

Words like *home and love* fell right out of my head because there was nowhere for them to go.

"Wanna go down to the beach?" I stood up on stiff morning legs.

"Sure," she said, and we made our way through the streets gone green and gold with light.

Kriel spread out a blanket and opened a plastic bag of crystals and wire. We made jewellery like patients in a psychiatric hospital, slow and methodical, shutting out the world with the soothing task. Idly chattering about what we'd do later, Kriel told me how she would get on a bus the next day or something.

We sat on the hot sand in wind that smelled of oil and garbage and salt, listening to the seagulls scream at the strolling crowds, the bustle and colour as permanent as the ocean. "Have you heard from Half-Peach since they went away?" Kriel asked.

"Nah," I said, toying absently with loose beads scattered on the blanket. I had resigned myself to the fact that I probably wouldn't see them again.

But Kriel was suddenly grinning at me, palm trees casting shadowy stripes across her cheeks. "Turn around," she said.

I squinted into the sun, shielding my eyes. Was that the silhouette of a straw hat? I got to my feet.

It was Half-Peach with a shiny blue bicycle. I ran across the sand and held them out at arm's length so I could look them over.

"When you didn't come find me, I knew I had to come back," they said, shrugging like it wasn't a big deal. "You really are a home bum."

"But I knew you'd be back."

"Where is everyone?" The beach, though packed with

skateboarders and hippies and tourists, felt empty of our friends.

"I dunno," I said. "Jay and Alex went to San Diego, Twist is back at his mom's and the others … who knows. Dead concerts and exoduses to South America, full moon gatherings in Arizona."

We wandered over to Big Daddy's and found Nate sitting on the sidewalk having a smoke. "Feels like everyone's gone," he said. "I thought you'd left too."

"Not yet," I said. Half-Peach wheeled the bike over to the restaurant window and ordered a hot dog. I sat down beside Nate, took his cigarette.

He lowered his voice. "Are you and Half-Peach going away together?"

"I think so," I said, and realized I was full of hope and plans. It was noisy around Big Daddy's. Rock 'n' roll blared from the skate park, rollerbladers sped past singing, gulls cried for pizza crusts, tourists pushed into each other competing for photographs, peddlers hollered about their hustles and wares, a juggler spat fire at the sky. It felt good to be going. "Do you want to come?"

"All right," Nate said.

Goodbye Glitter City, goodbye beaches and palm trees, scandal and crime, hustles and dumpsters, cardboard signs, boardwalks crowded with cops and babies, dogs and celebrities, film crews, sunglasses, eyes and hands.

You cannot walk out of Los Angeles; it isn't made that way. When we wanted to go, we had to take a bus out to a train station. We lolled around the blacktop outside Union Station, soaking up the heat blaring from the asphalt, our faces brown with dirt and sun.

It was Nate who went inside the station to ask how to leave LA. He was the pragmatic one, the most normal-looking one. Half-Peach with suspenders and no shirt, banjo slung over one shoulder with a chiffon scarf strap, a piece of prairie grass all the way from Humboldt County hanging from their bottom lip. Me with my silk pajamas, my pretty but ridiculous shoes and just something about my expression that made going incognito impossible. So we sent in Nate with his T-shirt and jeans, his simple country face.

The palms gave no shade; they were only there for decoration, like every person around me with an oyster-white convertible, wearing leather and cashmere, red lipstick and shampooed hair. A well of luxury that never ran dry.

I picked up cigarette butts from the ground and smoked them, but first ran a lighter over the filters to sterilize them. I wasn't an idiot.

Nate came back out reciting ticket prices we couldn't afford, so Half-Peach put their straw hat upside down to catch any falling cash and I played my guitar with the sticker along the bottom that said *Bend Space Time.*

Finally we left, going first through Compton. Ugly tongues of bleached concrete and more lonely palm trees, fast food restaurants and strip malls.

We were headed south, that's all I knew. Slab City because Half-Peach had a friend there. They had a friend here, there and everywhere. We got off the line in Long Beach. Men swaggered past us, holding on to the waistbands of their pants. I knew they couldn't chase us without losing their jeans, but I didn't want to be pursued by men in their underwear either. Half-Peach said Long Beach was nice everywhere but that street corner. Nate said he'd rather keep moving.

In Orange County, under the ripe purple sky, the three of us sat on the curb, washed up in an oasis of concrete and gas stations. The street lights made the surrounding darkness unplumbable.

Half-Peach went into the gas station to find out how far we were from Ocean Beach. Nate and I sat with our legs outstretched, listening to the highway sounds.

"I want to know where I stand," he said when the cars quieted down.

"Where you stand?"

"I only came because of you. I want to be where you are." He scowled to keep his composure.

"Nate ... you're a great friend," I said at last, kicking my feet out of my shoes and examining my toes poking from my socks. I never told Half-Peach how I'd come to know Nate, and if they suspected anything more than friendship, they never said. Half-Peach was a human puppy. But Nate, burly, handsome, typical, would want to return to his hometown, and I wouldn't go with him.

Half-Peach I could keep in my pocket, and when we left each other, as I already knew we would, it would be with finality because they couldn't leave a mark on me the way Leo had. The way Nate would.

Nate stood up, nodding as if he had just reached an agreement with himself. And Half-Peach came out of the gas station, whistling a tune.

We walked along the side of the highway under the fermented sky, trucks snarling past in a rush. The road rolled beneath our feet.

Half-Peach said they knew a strip of bushes in the highway's median we could sleep inside.

"I stayed here last time I made my way down," they called over the cars bathing us in accusatory light, honking as we made our way on the sandy shoulder of the road.

We had to wait until the road was empty and then run across the asphalt to the median between highways. The bushes were thick enough that when we crawled inside, the world was shut out. We weren't the first to use the shelter—tin camping pots, old sweaters, condom wrappers and cardboard told us that.

Nate lay at one end of the bush, Half-Peach slept in the middle and I was down at the other end. Nobody said anything as we rolled out our sleeping bags. Headlights and car noise cut through the camp all night, and I knew that because I stayed awake and listened.

The grey light of dawn woke us, or maybe it was the cars, roaring as if we were in the mouth of some machine. Half-Peach was up and giddy already, wanting to take us to a fast food place down the road they remembered.

The three of us sat at a picnic table outside, eating quietly until Little Wing dunked her nose into my hot coffee. The distraction was welcome in the strained silence. Half-Peach obliviously talking to an old woman in a wheelchair, pointing at the clouds and asking how long the weather would hold, bragging about their travels and where we were headed next. I could feel Nate staring at me.

After we finished eating, we headed to the shoulder of the road to hitch a ride to San Diego. A soldier named Bill pulled over for us, and I sat in the front seat. He was in uniform and said he had just gotten back from Afghanistan.

"You were fighting the terrorists?" I said by way of conversation.

The soldier shrugged, his face on the road. "Doesn't matter. I gotta take care of my mom and brother. Nobody else will." He turned up the radio so no one could speak again.

When we arrived in Ocean Beach, we found Alex and Jay dancing on the sand. Alex warned us the police here weren't as tolerant with dirty hippies as they'd been in Los Angeles. "Already saw the cops beat the living shit out of some old man earlier today. Ask around. They turned his face to pulp. I hope you have friends you can stay with. This place is not safe at night."

"Don't worry, I have a friend here," Nate told us as we fled the open twilight. He walked on ahead with Half-Peach. Ocean Beach was quaint and wonderful. It didn't seem unsafe. The town was quiet as we strolled the main drag, past tiny, colourful shops and lampposts, antique stores and taco joints, the smell of the waves behind us. Here the palm trees seemed longer, skinnier, as if they thrived on the fresh air, away from major freeways and industrial waste. I pretended I was just another tourist on a sightseeing trip, headed back to my hotel, ready for another full day. How fun.

Nate led us to a white apartment building, up clattering steel stairs to the top apartment. A bearded man answered the door, grinning, hugging Nate. He was older than us, and clean. "Come on in," he said, opening the door and pulling Nate into the apartment. "I'm Luke." It was the kind of place where one took one's shoes off immediately, which we did, leaving them on a bamboo mat. Luke told us he studied Chinese medicine. His wife Sara, a student, was still at school.

"Do you want some chocolate hemp milk?" he asked and set out a lacquered tray with glasses. Lighting a joint the size of his thumb, he passed it around until we were all lying on the carpet. I breathed in the smells of the home: nag champa and clean laundry, pot smoke, the oaky smell of the coffee table. The walls were the same colour as red wine, pillows everywhere. On the coffee table was a big hardcover book Luke had printed himself from photographs of his honeymoon with Sara, a trip along the coast. "We drove all the way up the One," he said, smiling as he recalled his secret memories. He was in love. He put on a Coltrane record and read the I Ching to me, but I was stoned, nothing stuck.

He let us put our sleeping bags on his living room floor but said Sara had to work all week so we could only stay one night.

The next morning, Half-Peach, Nate and I packed up our things, left a thank-you note for Luke and crept into the grey dawn. We went down to the sand and sat there talking about what we might do now. Nate, who'd been quiet, suddenly stood up and grabbed his things, as if he'd made a silent decision.

"I'm going to get a coffee," he said. But as he walked away, I knew he wasn't coming back.

The nights in Ocean Beach were lonely, the days quiet. Ocean Beach was not an offshoot of a sprawling urban mass, as Venice Beach had been. The hours crawled by. Where were Alex and Jay? We looked for them on the beach, but they had gone.

Half-Peach wanted to ride around on the city bus; they said we would find another friend. It was night now, late, and I was tired. As we rode through the dark streets as if in some sort of purgatory, a woman sitting across the aisle from us kept trying to catch my eye. Finally she leaned over, putting her reading glasses on top of her grey hair. "You kids going somewhere in particular?"

I looked at Half-Peach. They shrugged.

A comma of friendliness surfaced near the corner of her mouth. "Listen, I never do this, but would it be all right if I get you all a room at my hotel? Here, let's get off at the next stop, that's me."

She pulled the bell cord and we stood together, Half-Peach and me obediently following her down from the bus and along the sidewalk toward the neon chain hotel where she was staying. The promise of a fresh, clean bed and hot shower surfaced like a lighthouse in the dark.

When we got to the lobby, Little Wing peeked her head out of my shirt.

"I didn't realize you were carrying a critter around with you," the woman cried, giving Little Wing's ears a scratch. "Don't let the hotel people see her, or they'll charge my card."

She paid at the front desk and said we were her niece and nephew from out of town. The clerk in his polyester uniform swiped the card and did not seem to care one way or the other who we were. She signed June Halliday on the receipt.

June led us to our room like we might run off, shepherding us along with her arms held out, handing us the plastic key only once we'd reached the door. She had the watery eyes of a mother, her tissue-paper skin crinkled with private worries. She smelled of drugstore lotion. She unlocked our door herself but stopped us before we went in.

"I had a daughter," she said, touching my arm. "She ran off. Over ten years ago." The hallway lights caught the dust of her eyeshadow. "Wherever she is, I hope someone is taking care of her too. Goodnight."

For a minute I let myself think of my mother and how she had the same tense insistence, the eyes of a woman with children. But when I went into the clean, dark room, I put those thoughts away.

"It's a miracle," Half-Peach said, jumping on the bed.

I stood in the hot shower and it was in fact a miracle. The sensation of hot water on skin, of being cleansed, the sheer luxury of being able to take care of my body. I soaked my hard muscles, breathed steam into my lungs, rinsed the dirt and grease from my hair, scrubbed my face with a rough washcloth, lathered my limbs in fragrant suds, watched the water run the road off me.

When I came out wrapped in a terry cloth bathrobe, I felt lottery ticket rich. I slipped between the blanket and a cool sheet, a mattress beneath my sore bones. Half-Peach opened the window a crack because it was hard to fall asleep without breathing the open air. We put on a black and white movie and Little Wing curled up on the foot of the bed, almost as if it were a permanent thing, this night. I fell asleep in seconds to the sound of Half-Peach murmuring bedtime stories of Slab City, the painted Bethlehem in the dirt, with the landmark called Salvation Mountain. I thought it was foolish to name a landmark after salvation—a mountain was permanent, and salvation was not.

Salvation Mountain

I woke up in the tarp, sweating already from the morning sun. The light through the blue plastic cast everything in blue, my skin, my hands. I was a mermaid at the bottom of the Salton Sea.

Half-Peach was already up and pulling suspenders over bare brown shoulders. "Angel doesn't know I'm coming. I can't wait to see her face."

We strolled along the desert road, past pale green sage bushes, cracked stretches of white earth bleached by the sun. Downtown Slab City was alive with activity, crowded with a cluster of trailers and lean-tos, people running around with wood and hammers, calling to each other, lugging buckets, carting food. There was a dining hall crowded with old men playing checkers at tables covered in plastic tablecloths. Half-Peach said, "You can buy coffee in Styrofoam cups, but it's a bit of a Slab City controversy."

Off to the side of the road was the Range, identified by a hand-painted sign. A stage had been built up out of the dust and decorated in antlers and patio lanterns, flanked by low couches and plastic chairs, empty in the daytime. At night there'd be performances, Half-Peach told me. I imagined grizzled old men with electric guitars wailing lonely melodies out across the desert. The heat of the morning rippled and buzzed.

Big slabs of cement checkered the baked white dirt. On almost every slab was a trailer or a tarp-tent, a ramshackle structure of pipes, plastic and boards. Dogs ran loose, barking at the sky. A truck drove by carrying a giant junk sculpture in the back—plastic Santa Clauses, pink flamingos, hula hoops.

We passed a skate park, a cement slab covered in plywood ramps where a few shirtless boys flew against the sun, dreadlocked hair scattering behind them. The clap of their skateboard wheels echoed across the empty rim of the desert. Reggae music blasted into the oppressive heat. Nine o'clock on a January morning and I was already sunburned. The smell of my sweat came up around me.

Behind the skate park was a long orange and brown striped trailer. The slab it rested on was messy with a flimsy table, a dozen folding chairs, a plaid couch and a hand-painted sign that said *Karma Kitchen*. Half-Peach went up to the trailer and pulled open the tin door. I followed them inside, squinting my eyes in the gloom. A loamy stench of pot smoke, unwashed sheets and carpet dust came on strong. Our heads brushed the ceiling.

"Scooter, look who's back. And on my birthday!" Her voice raspy like a crow's. She was sunk into the couch but stiffly pulled herself up when we came through the door. The wood-panelled walls were buried behind photographs, crystals on strings, dangling owl feathers, doll heads. An entire wolf skin hung behind the couch.

"Take a box of celery, they're outside. Bring one to Tumbleweed, he don't leave his trailer now that he got an internet girlfriend. You wanna use his computer, just put your name on the paper outside his door." Angel sat back into the couch, pulling Half-Peach down with her. She extracted a glass pipe shaped like a dragon from the pocket of her skirt and pushed a tuft of marijuana into the bowl. When she fired it up, the dank skunk smell burst forth into the narrow space. Her long hair was the same colour as the landscape, goldish brown and grey. "I know Half-Peach here," she choked, exhaling smoke from the gaps in her teeth, "but I haven't got the pleasure with you." Her hand was strong and broad as a man's. When we shook, she tugged on my hand a little, getting me to sit in a chair beside her.

"When did you get in?" Half-Peach asked Angel, accepting the pipe.

"About a few months ago. Me and Scoot were up in Portland again." She leaned forward and shouted down the trailer hallway, "Scooter, get out here!"

There was the sound of someone pushing his way through clutter, a chair being scraped, papers falling, and Scooter presented himself in the living room. He was so tall he had to crouch. His face was long like a hound dog's, his hair yellow-white, curling out from under a safari hat.

"Hi, Half-Peach, hi, new girl," he said and sat down in the corner La-Z-Boy. He turned on the television in its heavy wooden case and even though the sound was down, he took refuge in staring at the screen.

Angel turned to me. Her eyes were round and yellow as a wolf's. "You gonna be okay with gas-jugging? The less ugly you are, the more responsibility you get. Show that little face around Niland and you'll come back here loaded down with more gas and canned goods than you can carry. Everybody gotta do their part."

Half-Peach put their hand on my bare knee. Angel spoke of my face as plain as if she was speaking of the sky being blue, but I did not feel pride. A pretty face could not be earned and it was as fleeting as everything else.

Little Wing snored on the carpet. The responsibility of being a girl had followed me here, to this free place.

Tumbleweed gifted us with a little trailer of our own. It was the kind of camper meant to fit in the back of a pickup truck, only the thing was propped up on wooden blocks between the trailer he lived in and Angel's.

Half-Peach and I sat on Angel's plaid couch and watched Tumbleweed get it ready for us. We kept calling over, "Are you sure you don't need help?" and a hand would poke through the door or window, flapping at us to dismiss the offer.

He pulled junk out of the trailer all afternoon. It looked like he'd been using the thing as his garbage can. He stumped back and forth from the slab to the bleached weeds, throwing out lone socks, toilet scrubbers, phone books, frying pans, a hamster cage.

"Every man needs to face the trash he accumulates and clean it up," he said. I think that's what he said. It was hard to catch his words. His mouth, caved-in from toothlessness, was covered in a nest of moustache and beard.

The little trailer still wasn't empty at nightfall—door open, leftover junk dribbled from its depths onto the ground.

Angel let us sleep on the couch on her slab. We had to lie on our sides to both fit, but it was more comfortable than the ground. Half-Peach was small, but still bigger than I was. My head tucked beneath their chin, Little Wing pressed between us like a conjoined heart. Minutes like these locked me down to the earth. I was glad to have the protection of Half-Peach. I was not ready to be alone in the desert. And it was nice to have a friend.

We were specks beneath the great stage of desert stars. I peeked out from our nest on the scratchy sofa. The sky was a dome above us, loaded and heavy with light. I had never seen a sky like that before, electric and spherical, almost visibly spinning around. The cosmos spread above us like one vast and infinite storyboard.

Half-Peach began talking about Venice Beach, their jaw making the words touch the top of my skull. "Remember when I went to Humboldt County for a couple weeks and I didn't think I was coming back?"

I said I remembered.

Their hot fingers restlessly drummed my ribcage, their talk speeding up a bit, as if they were worried about getting the words out in time. "I didn't think I was gonna come back. I didn't think I'd see you again. Before I left, I gave Bench Lady a message and told her to pass it along to you."

In the darkness, I could see Bench Lady, a fixture stationary as a palm tree. A mess of turquoise rings along her fingers. Bench Lady with her pink lipstick and red cowboy boots, straw hat with a big plastic sunflower on the brim.

"She never said anything to me." I rolled onto my back with Half-Peach curled against me.

Looking into the depths of the stars, it was easy to pretend we were flying through space at lightspeed, off to some new galaxy.

Half-Peach shrugged, as much as they could in the way we were lying. "Weird. Bench Lady was always so reliable about passing things along." Half-Peach was continually surprised when the workings of the known world broke down. They took everything around them for granted, expecting it to remain static for their sanity. When things shifted and changed, I could see their mind, pure and fragile, trying to reconcile these new uncertainties.

"What was the message? We're here now. Might as well tell me yourself," I said to the inky dark.

The pause was long as the sky over the landscape of scattered trailers and concrete. "I wanted her to tell you ..." They drew in a breath and let it out, an impatient puff against the side of my neck. "I told her to tell you ..." The warm fingers drumming my ribs again. "... The message was that ... it was I love you. I mean the message was. It was I love you. I wanted her to tell you that I was in love with you. That I am in love with you."

The desert was so quiet I could hear the coyotes singing their pups to sleep. I could hear laughter coming from nowhere. I could hear the whine of a motorbike coming all the way from town, the sound of someone trying to get away. Half-Peach's hair against my cheek smelled of asphalt, which was the smell of the road in the afternoon. And I said it back because in that moment, already moving away, it was true.

We piled all of our stuff into the little trailer, scarves and guitars and a rag doll that someone had given me back in

Venice Beach. I hung up our road map with its inked-on routes and detours. We stuck glow-in-the-dark stickers on the walls. I hadn't realized I was tired until I lay down. We were like the old snowbirds who came in their creaking trailers trying to warm their bones. Our sleeping bags still smelled like salt and sand from the Pacific Ocean, and I did miss the coast. I tried not to think about the word *landlocked*.

Even in this wild place, we fell into a routine, washing the rags of our clothes in the hot springs, tidying our trailer and promenading the cracked white earth.

After a few days, we headed into Niland to apply for food stamps, which took up an entire afternoon. Half-Peach and me in a government building so overly air-conditioned that my teeth hurt. I held Little Wing in my arms and five Mexican women who spoke no English gathered around me to stroke her ears. None of us needed words to appreciate the puppy.

On a little television in the corner, a fuzzy instructional video about the benefits of having a vasectomy played. Half-Peach sat low in the plastic chair.

Finally a woman wearing a square purple suit called their name and told them they had been approved for Electronic Benefits Transfer, but that we'd have to come back to pick up the paperwork in a day or two; it was mailed in from El Centro. Because I was Canadian, I didn't even exist in their paperwork. I waited around until it was over, and then we hitchhiked back to the slabs.

Leonard had built Salvation Mountain with his own hands. It looked like a wedding cake, a pile of paint, a lumpy hillock of folk art and bible verses. *GOD IS LOVE* was painted beneath a white cross that shot up at the sky. *Say Jesus I'm a Sinner, please come upon my body and into my heart,* was painted in white letters inside a massive heart on the side of the hill.

Half-Peach and I walked over in a blistering white morning, Little Wing running along behind us. My eyes squinting in the sun. Leonard circled the periphery of his work in a T-shirt and cargo shorts, his white hair almost invisible against the sky. Tourists took photos, wanted to talk to Leonard.

"Can we go inside?" I asked Half-Peach, who was not as enthusiastic about the installation as I was. They'd already crawled all over the thing.

"It's possible," they said. They went over to say hello to Leonard, flanked by the eager inner-city pilgrims who'd driven from San Diego.

I went into the painted cave alone. It was like climbing inside a psychedelic tulip: tree branches and hay bales painted up with bible verses and flowers, blue and white stripes and golden stairs, scrolls covered in the name of Jesus. It was cooler inside. Little Wing's claws clicked across the painted floor. The sun came through the tree branch roof, the chinks in the walls, inside this vivid painted heart. In the centre of the cave were trees painted with dollops of red flowers, and under the paint they looked petrified, like cakey stalagmites. At the back of the domed space, a car door was embedded into the walls as if it had been swallowed, sucked into the sculpture. If I stood still, the colours moved around me like a stop-motion Bible story. *Jesus loves you, you love Jesus*, was painted on the door to nowhere.

My cooling sweat made me itchy and cold. I had been raised Methodist. Jesus and his love felt as two-dimensional as the paintings in the man-made cave.

I stepped back into the light, shielding my eyes from the glare of the sun.

"You ready to go?" Half-Peach called to me.

On the way back from Salvation Mountain, Half-Peach and I went visiting. Moth lived in an empty silo on the edges of Slab City, beyond Salvation Mountain.

"Where'd he come from?" I asked. We crossed the cracked-open desert, Little Wing racing along the edges of the dunes. Mid-afternoon sun came down like a violent fist; there was no air. The birds didn't sing, they screamed.

"I have no idea," Half-Peach said, pushing up their straw hat and using the back of their hand to wipe sweat off their forehead, leaving behind a stripe of grime. "Make sure the hawks don't get her."

I looked over at Little Wing. Her pink tongue hanging out like a ribbon. Her glossy black fur had gone matte with dust. She trotted along unleashed and content, eyeballs rolling, a foreign delicacy in a predator's landscape.

Moth stood in the doorway as if he'd been waiting for us. He wore long skirts and had a beard like a bird's nest down to his bellybutton. "Greetings," he said. His hair hung down in long strings, his wide eyes blue as an electric shock. On his face was an expression of perpetual disbelief, as if he couldn't understand where he'd wound up and what he was seeing. He could have been twenty-two or forty-two. It was impossible to tell.

The inside of the silo was cool, almost damp with shadow. A wooden platform at the far end of the space had a sleeping bag on it. Old calendars were taped all over the wall, going back as far as 1972.

Moth said, "It has been a tough year at the slabs." His voice was rich and theatrical. He sounded as if he were speaking from a stage. Emptying a canteen of water into a dented pot, he settled it on a Bunsen burner with care. "Angel says she has some celery up at the kitchen for me. After this, let us head there together."

Half-Peach sat cross-legged on the dirt floor. The silo bounced our voices around in a circle, so we had to listen to the words from our mouths twice. "How long you been in the slabs for, Moth?" Half-Peach asked because they knew I'd want to know. They were good to me that way.

"Long enough to get the lay of the land." Moth poured tea into three mugs and handed them around. I discreetly wiped dust from the rim of my cup before taking a sip of the flavourless water. "There was a Hollywood film made here a few years ago. You weren't around then, Peach. Everyone made over a hundred dollars being movie extras. No one knew what to do with that kind of money, of course, so things became debaucherous and more violent than usual. I, myself, am a sober person, naturally. Money is not a wise thing to introduce in this place. It certainly changed the topography. Now, more recently there has been talk of a serial killer. But this is their territory, after all. It is probably associated with the men who come here to cook methamphetamine in the summertime ... Did you know I am from Milwaukee?" Moth made a sweeping gesture with his hand, which seemed to indicate the length of the land he'd crossed to get here. "Well, I am. I am from Milwaukee. I would say I have been here four, maybe five years? I spend my summers in this silo and it is like living in an oven. Being cooked alive. But then, it is worse out there. In the summer, it is silent as a tomb. Everything is buried by the sand. No cops, no law. You take one look at the land, and you want to die. The sun is relentless. I see what happens, but I keep it to myself. No one will get a story from me." His blue eyes burned as they roamed the corrugated aluminum walls and came to rest on my face. He took a long, slow slurp from his cup. "Half-Peach is the only one who comes to visit. Everyone else calls me the curse of the slabs. Because I never leave. I only watch. No one wants to be watched out here. But who am I? I am only a man running around the desert in a dress." And Moth suddenly broke into the dance of a court jester, water slopping from his cup and making mud of the ground.

The three of us crossed over the desert together so Moth could get his box of celery. "Angel is the only one who gives a damn about me getting my three squares," he said. He walked ahead of us and didn't turn around to speak. His lengths of skirt swirled around his legs, brushing the tops of his sneakers. Half-Peach, Little Wing and I followed quietly. I'd learned back in Los Angeles that fewer words were better than plenty. I said nothing. It had kept me safe so far.

"Her real name is Seraphim. Did you know that? Seraphim. But she wanted to go by Angel. She told me people would be too stupid to pronounce her name. But perhaps she underestimates the people here. I know she underestimates me."

Scooter wasn't around when we got back to the Karma Kitchen. We could see his long back in the ripples of the heat, walking away with a shotgun slung over his shoulder.

Angel was sunk into the couch when we came through the trailer door, her hands shaking away. She told us Scooter had gone to catch some hares, and she would make gumbo on Friday. Friday was Family Dinner, and the big table would be set for anyone around the slabs who wanted to partake. Angel volunteered Half-Peach and me for dishwashing duty.

"MS is bad today, kiddos," she said. " Moth, go on and light my pipe for me." Moth expertly packed Angel's pipe and brought it gently to her puckered mouth, scritching the lighter to a flame. Angel's shaking slowed and she leaned back, beatific and spent. "We gotta go back to Oregon soon. Thank god for the weed. Poor man's medicine." I opened my mouth to ask her why she wasn't going to a doctor, but remembered before I spoke. The privileges of Canadian healthcare were far behind me now.

Half-Peach lay on the rug like a child. Moth sat beside Angel on the couch, holding her hands in his own. She opened one eye at me, to watch me lean against the door. "My twin girls would have been about your age," Angel said. We waited for her to say more, but she changed the subject.

"I never told you about my Jewish grandfather, did I." Her voice, low and husky, brought out the story as if she were sitting beside a fire drawing pictures from the smoke. "My Hopi grandmother," she began, "married a Jew. You sure I never told this one?" Half-Peach and Moth shook their heads, but they would've said no anyway just to have Angel charm them with one of her stories. "He was a Jew escaping Germany. This was in the middle of the war, nobody knew about the death camps. Well, everyone claimed they didn't know. But if you had any sense of smell, you knew. Anyway, he was escaping from all that. When these Jews came over, they needed someone to speak for them, they needed someone to come forward on the docks and say, 'That Jew is mine.' He'd already hustled his way out of his home, leaving behind everything. Who knows what happened to him back there. He never said. He made it onto a boat, somehow dodged the submarines. He made it to America. And now he was going to need someone to speak for him so that he could stay. My grandmother was working at a nurse's college and she and all the other nurses knew about these Jews coming over on a boat, so they went down to the docks to get these men. War duty included more than just bandaging wounds and knitting socks. When that first Jew came down out of the boat, whoever was in charge yelled, 'Whose man is this?' My grandmother stepped up and said, 'That's my man.' They were married right there on the docks. That was their wedding. And wouldn't you know it, that man had been a jeweller back in Germany. He'd sewn his clothes with jewels." She pressed her lips together and closed her eyes again. "But America is expensive," she said.

The next morning, I went over to Tumbleweed's trailer to check my emails. It was a ritual I wasn't yet ready to untether from. There were a couple of men ahead of me in the lineup. Tumbleweed was off in town somewhere, and we stood around in the shade of the trailer, waiting for the rattling sound of his truck.

When he did pull up, he shooed all the men away. "Ladies first, fellas, ladies first." The men shrugged good-naturedly and went loping off across the sand like a couple of stray coyotes. "Come on in, sweetie, I got some instant coffee from town." Tumbleweed patted down his wild grey mat of hair and ushered me into the dark tunnel of his trailer. It smelled like canned soup and aftershave.

Sitting down at the padded bench behind the fold-down table, I watched Tumbleweed clattering around the kitchen counter, making us mugs of coffee. Then he sat across from me and opened up the laptop, thick as a military computer full of secrets.

"Cops don't know we got internet out here." Tumbleweed chewed and swallowed his words when he spoke, touched the side of his nose and winked at me. His face a web of wrinkles. "Gotta check in with my girlfriend, then you can do what you gotta." He started typing away on the keys, the light from the screen settling in deep reliefs on his skinny face.

"Where's your girlfriend?" I curled my fingers around the mug. It was reassuring to have a cup of coffee in this place. The routine made me feel calm.

"In Rhode Island. She's a thirty-two-year-old Virgo." But his attention was divided, and his words were in Rhode Island with his internet girlfriend.

"Think she'll ever come out to Slab City?"

"Lord no. She'll stay in this little screen, right where I want her."

"This is about as close to a Third World country as you're going to get without crossing the border to Brown Town," the snowbird told his wife. They were holding hands, but lazily, dangling fingers between the seats. She had red lacquered fingernails that glinted in the sun, both of them with suburban haircuts and matching track suits. They were staying at a campsite past Niland but liked to drive around and marvel at the weirdness of Slab City. That was how they'd come to pick up Half-Peach and me, hitching to the grocery store. The behemoth trailer slowly pulled to the side and waited for us to climb aboard.

The streets in town had names like Isis and International, and they ran flat along the earth. The houses were nothing but trailers penned in by chain-link. A few dogs ran along the road, chasing after nothing. The trees were akin to palms but were not the long, skinny beauties of Los Angeles—the trunks out here were short and shaggy. There was no grass. Nothing was green except for a few brave leaves clinging to the remains of a skeletal crop of bushes. The white sky and the savagery of the sun.

A many-pillared building, which had probably once been a bank, stood abandoned and covered in spray paint near the railroad tracks. Our driver slowed down to whistle through his teeth at this. His wife whispered, "Can you imagine?" because she could not.

The thing that struck me most about the town was the trash. The yards were stacked high with random garbage and rusted appliances, rebar and loose wood. For people who were supposed to be poor, I'd never seen such towering heaps of stuff.

It was even worse out at Slab City. The slab-dwellers called it "desert shopping," and you could decorate an entire trailer that way. Half-Peach and I had gone poking around the Free Slab once, out on the fringes of Slab City, a necklace of forgotten things. Pea-green squares of carpet, statues with missing heads, children's books and playing cards, polyester disco pants, mildewed shirts with Peter Pan collars, scorched lampshades, shopping carts, cat kennels, rotting teddy bears, warped dishes, ruined chairs. Piles and piles of cast-off possessions tangled up in the dry bushes, burned white by the unrelenting sun.

We got dropped off on the side of the highway near the Buckshot Diner and walked along the hot road until we reached the grocery store, displaying a wilted American flag. We sat down under the awning, the cement cold under my butt. Half-Peach pulled the banjo off their back and put their straw hat on the ground upside down, strumming some folk songs, familiar things that everyone liked to hum.

The men who walked past us into the store were rough and dust-covered, creases around their eyes white where the sun hadn't reached. They looked us over where we sat in our flowered rags and tossed down a wrinkled buck, mostly because they knew we needed to be paid to go away.

Venom and Roxy finally arrived in Slab City. Half-Peach and I had come across them in San Diego, at a city fair. Venom had been begging men sweetly for cigarettes and spare change. The four of us spent the day walking around the city and picking through dumpsters.

Half-Peach had said we were headed for the desert and invited the couple along, but they were in the middle of some scam, Venom rolling men for wallets or something, and said they'd catch up later.

And now they had come. Half-Peach and I were peeling potatoes around the table at the Karma Kitchen when we saw them walking across the desert, wearing the same clothes as last time.

"Slab City is crazy," Venom sang, coming across the hot cement toward us, her lanky arms open wide. Even here, she wore a grubby winter toque pulled low over her forehead, her long white legs streaming from a pair of tiny denim shorts.

"You all wanna head over there?" Roxy asked excitedly, his thin smile interrupted by several clunky lip rings. His blond hair swept sideways across his forehead like he was stuck forever in a strong wind. He gestured behind him at the skate park, where the Rolling Stones blasted so loudly we had to shout. The skateboarders leaned against handmade ramps, snorting drugs off the ridges of their knuckles.

"We gotta do meal prep for Angel. This is her slab," Half-Peach said, flipping a bald, wet potato into a bowl, irritated. I could tell by the way their eyebrows gathered. Half-Peach had great respect for the way things were done in Slab City. "How about you come with us to Niland after. We have to get more groceries for the dinner tonight."

"Man, we just came from there," Venom whined. "I wanna explore the slabs." Her restless eyes contrasted against the quiet kitchen slab. The air smelled like burnt earth, like melting plastic.

"If you help us, you'll get fed," I told them.

Roxy and Venom made many shrugging, reluctant gestures and then sat down to help us finish peeling the potatoes.

We headed down the road to the fire station that doubled as a food bank. The heat of the afternoon was so heavy, it made me want to close my eyes. It made a terrible pressure inside my head.

The fire station was closed. The chain-link fence had a padlock on it and the parking lot was empty. It smelled of melting tar. The white building with its plain lettering, *Niland Fire District*, seemed like everything else in town— desolate and left behind. It filled me with a sense of eeriness, as if all the people in the world had moved away while I was sleeping.

"Y'all lookin' for something?" The voice came from behind us. We turned to see a blond woman leaning out of her car window, snapping bubble gum.

"Isn't this a food bank?" I asked her.

"Only sometimes. And this ain't one of them times. You all tryin' to get some food, go on to the grocery store."

"We're hobos. We want free shit. We can't pay for anything," yelled Roxy, turning his pockets inside out to show that they were empty.

The woman pulled herself back into her car and rolled her window up halfway for protection. "You slab peoples. If you're lookin' for handouts, go on to the Immaculate Heart of Mary. They got a little brown woman who gives out food. But you people probably already ran her dry looking for your ... *free shit.*" She made a big production of driving away, tires squealing.

"Fuck you, lady," Venom hollered after the car, raising her middle finger. She and Roxy cackled and high-fived each other.

Half-Peach looked over at me with the same expression Little Wing had sometimes, vaguely ashamed. "We can't go back to the Karma Kitchen empty-handed," they said, voice low so only I could hear.

I nodded, drawing shapes in the dust with the toe of my shoe. How often we were thrown in with people we did not like but had to suffer. We were just here. I felt pale to the point of invisibility, a fly on the wall, a follower. We only went along to see what would happen to us next.

"How about you and Roxy go to the grocery store and play some guitar," I said. "Me and Venom will suss out the church." It was important to have some semblance of a plan, a map to guide us even through our own spontaneity. Otherwise we would disappear.

Half-Peach said this was a smart idea and walked away with Roxy to Main Street. Venom and I headed down Niland Avenue, a diagonal street cutting through the neighbourhood, toward the Catholic church.

We mostly walked in silence, Venom sometimes remarking on a tall pile of trash. Her legs were impossibly long. She was model-beautiful but seemed terrified by it. She kept her arms crossed over her chest, only uncrossing them when she needed her hands.

We came to the church, the only building on its side

of the street. It was a sand-coloured building with arched windows along the front, two haggard trees posted on either side and a little wrought iron fence around it. The yard had no grass. A low-slung building beside it seemed to be a residence of some kind, and when Venom and I crossed the bald yard, a Mexican woman came out to meet us, quick as a bird coming out of a clock.

"*Sí?*"

Venom went and slouched on a bench in the yard. "We need food, lady."

I wanted to apologize to the woman, but I couldn't speak Spanish.

The woman shrugged. Her skin knew what to do with the sunlight. We were pasty and sunburned beside her. I mimed eating, bringing my empty hands to my mouth.

She nodded at me, understanding, but glared back at Venom, sprawled out lazy as a rag doll.

I smiled at her. "Please?" I wished I had something to give in exchange. Needing charity was a constant shame.

With resignation the woman held up a finger, turned around and went back into the residence, shutting the door behind her. I sat on the bench beside Venom.

"I'm never going back to San Diego," she said, crossing her long legs, wrapping one behind the other like embracing swans. She conjured a limp cigarette from somewhere and lit it up, blowing the smoke hard into the stagnant air.

"Is that where you're from?" I asked. My mouth was so parched, the words sounded as if they were cracking. I never felt hydrated anymore. The heat had settled inside my bones.

"I guess. I live with my mom sometimes and my dad sometimes. I mean my other mom. My dad decided he wanted to become a woman. But man or woman, he was still an asshole. He was drunk literally all the time. He only spent money on makeup and clothes. I needed fucking glasses, and did I ever get them? I'm practically fucking blind. The last fight we got into, he threw me through the glass coffee table. Have you ever been thrown through a panel of glass? It's crazy, it's like being in the middle of an explosion. And afterwards you're all cut up. Obviously, I left. Now he can spend his money getting his fake tits. What does he know about growing up as a girl? Everyone celebrates him for his transformation, as if he's made the world a better place. But I'm still just a stupid girl. Anyway, I got Roxy and we're gonna keep moving along."

The Mexican woman came back out of the building and handed us a loaf of white bread and a can of soup. Then she made a shooing motion, sweeping us away with her hands.

We walked along the dirt road to the grocery store to get the others, Venom cradling the loaf of bread like a baby.

The next day, Half-Peach got their food stamps.

They ran up and down the aisles of the grocery store, filling the cart with handfuls and handfuls of chocolate bars, cake, candy, pancake mix.

When we came back outside, a rainstorm was nearly on top of us. The sky roiled with sudden clouds, and there we were with our armloads of food. We'd lost track of time in town, and nobody was on the road back to Slab City anymore. The smell of earth before the rain filled my nose. The wind was cold and laced with water.

"We better walk fast," warned Half-Peach. We went as quickly as we could down the dirt road, black clouds a heavy layer above our heads.

We got as far as the railroad tracks before the sky broke open, a sideways scream of a storm. The trees bent over. The horizontal rain flew, my hair plastered across my face. Half-Peach and I stood still in the middle of the flooded road. I wiped water from my eyes.

"Stay here," Half-Peach shouted over the roar of the storm. They left me with the bags and ran off to investigate an old shack. But it turned out to have no roof.

"What about the bank?" I yelled as they came jogging back, a soaked figure in the dark.

Bent over in the wind, we struggled toward the abandoned bank and ducked under its dripping awning. Our footsteps echoed on the concrete. Shadows hugged the spray-painted pillars, creating dark pools. The double doors were padlocked and chained shut. I pressed my ear to the wood and could hear singing or moaning, a terrible laughter coming from inside.

"Maybe we can wait out the storm?" I said hopefully, my voice reverberating off the empty stretches of cement. I wrapped my arms around my ribs, my skin wet and icy. I was only wearing a sundress. It had been so warm when we'd left.

We stood under the awning for a while, squinting out into the roaring downpour, scanning the storm for a pair of headlights or a break in the rain. I paced impatiently, my shoes squelching. We'd rested our grocery bags against the wall of the bank. I heard more laughter, almost like a hyena. The dampness crept into my limbs. My teeth chattered.

Half-Peach started saying something about how we might have to spend the night, but I interrupted, taunted by images of our warm, dry trailer back in the slabs. The cold made me savage and impatient. I'd been accused of being spoiled before—I'd been the only homeless person in Venice Beach to sneak into café bathrooms to brush my teeth.

"I'm going to knock on someone's door," I said. Beyond the pillars and the curtain of rain, I could see the twinkle of window lights coming from a trailer out there in the dark.

Half-Peach grabbed my arm. "This isn't the friendly slabs. People get shot for trespassing all the time."

"Whatever," I said and pulled free. I hadn't grown up with the threat of guns.

I ran across the road, ducking in the pelting rain, crossed an Astroturf lawn and knocked on the tin door. A yellow light came from the windows and a blare of bluegrass music. I knocked again, harder.

The whole trailer began to tremble with lumbering footsteps that stopped abruptly on the other side of the door. I could feel someone examining me from the narrow window.

Beyond the rushing roar of the rainstorm and the twanging chaos of bluegrass music, I heard the occupant yell, "Who the fuck's there?" Before I could say, the door wrenched violently open. Standing there in his underwear was a man with a body like a big ball of dough. I was eye-level with his broad, bald chest. He blinked down at me. Half-Peach came slinking across the road and crouched behind me. "I don't know you," he said stupidly. Then, "Come on, get out of the rain." He waddled back into the depths of the trailer, leaving the door open for us.

I stepped into the trailer, Half-Peach shuffling in behind me with the dripping bags of groceries. The man inserted himself back into a sunken sofa and continued to make his way through an eighteen-pack of beer. He'd turned down the stereo but not much.

"We were caught in the storm on our way back to Slab

City," I shouted over the music, sitting on the edge of a kitchen chair.

The man scratched his shaved head lazily. "Don't need to tell me where y'all were goin', can tell jest by lookin' atche. You all want a beer? My name's Junior." He sat up a bit and handed us each a warm beer. "You can sit here for a bit and dry off, but then you got to go. Can't have hippie kids crashing here. You do it and next thing I know, this place will be overrun with all your weirdo friends." He fell back against the couch cushions. I could smell the waves of barley coming off him and under that, a smell of something loamy, unwashed.

"Thanks for letting us in, anyway," Half-Peach said, popping open their can and taking a long haul on it. Now that I'd taken care of the situation, they were content as if we were sitting in our own living room.

Junior said, "Let's don't talk about it no more. I was jest having some beers anyways. This song," and he leaned forward to crank up the stereo again, hollering over the bluegrass, "reminds me of my daddy. He jest had a heart surgery and we don't know if he gon' make it."

A fiddle ballad whined from the speakers, and a man sang through his nose about the long and winding road of life, the loneliness of it, and the grace of God that gets man through.

Half-Peach stepped outside the trailer and pissed into the rain.

Junior lowered the music, looking me over beadily. "Where you from, girl?"

"Nova Scotia." It felt like a long way off now, the Atlantic Ocean, the East Coast. I instantly regretted telling Junior anything about myself. You gave people access, and suddenly they were pulling open your chest just to watch the way your heart beat.

"Don't know nothin' about that place," Junior stated plainly. "Were you my girlfriend, you wouldn't have to go back to no Novin Scotia." Half-Peach came back inside. Junior scowled and turned the music back up. "You all can sleep here, but I ain't makin' up a bed for you, you got to do it yourselves," he shouted.

While the two of them finished off the eighteen-pack and listened to songs that reminded Junior of his aunty, his brother and his childhood cat, he told us how he was in the military but had been discharged. He didn't say why. Junior said he'd been born and raised in Niland. He used to go explore the slabs when he was a boy, but now it was overrun with freaks and druggies, and we should get the hell out while we were still alive. Finally Junior said it was time for bed.

I stood up and began clearing off the kitchen table, which Junior told me folded down into a bed. The table was covered with old lamps missing their shades, lunch boxes, frying pans, damp towels, an empty laundry hamper and jeans that smelled like balls.

Junior came over. "Outta the way, girly, lemme do it." He swept everything onto the floor, folded the table down, threw the cushions over it and snapped a sheet across. "There. Bed's made."

"Can we offer you some groceries? I just got my food stamps," Half-Peach said.

Junior wouldn't accept any of it. "Forget it. I got some chocolate over there on the counter. You help yourself." Half-Peach grinned appreciatively. Junior continued, "You got to leave the way to the bathroom clear, 'cause in the night I pee. I also sleep naked. So when I climb up into my bed, don't you go peekin' at my ball sack." His bed was a bunk against the wall with a ladder leaning against it. It looked dangerously close to collapsing in the middle.

Junior snored like a dump truck. I lay there staring at the ceiling. Half-Peach slept beside me, peaceful as a pup.

In the morning, it was still raining. Junior gave us military-issued rain ponchos, and when we got back out on the road, a car picked us up right away.

Half-Peach and I, soaking in the hot springs in the early morning, the day grey and smudged. The pale whiskers of reedy grass seemed almost like privacy, but the hot springs were rarely empty, and we'd sat in the hot water for only five minutes before a scrawny little woman came wading through the brush toward us, dressed in a neon-pink bikini. She waved her hand in a salute, readjusting the towel around her neck. I could hear the *thwack* of her sandals as she came closer. She had the body of a sixteen-year-old but the face of a grandmother, her blond hair shorn around her ears.

"Hi all," she sang out, dropping her towel in the dirt and slipping down into the water, sleek as a minnow. She said her name was Pixie. Along behind her came her son, twenty-something, swim shorts low on his skinny hips. He had the exact same face as his mother, but less ravaged by time.

Sometimes in the morning Half-Peach and I didn't speak for hours. We were both so quiet. At first I resented having to chitchat with Pixie, but she filled the morning up with her chatter so I didn't have to speak anyway.

"That's my son, Keebler," she pointed at him as he climbed down into the spring with us. "We're townies. We don't live in the slabs, but I'm considering it, coming out here, being done with my taxes. We live in a piece-of-shit trailer in town. How does that wind up being expensive? Who knows. Keebler and I come out here all the time to get a soak and talk with the folks in Slab City; they're so weird and never from around here like me and Keebs. It's so strange! Furthest I've been is Los Angeles. Wish I had the money to live there. Keebler has a car though, and a job in El Centro. He takes care of me, don't you baby?" The woman had a voice like glucose-fructose. She busied herself rubbing mud along her skinny, freckled arms and across the deep wrinkles in her sun-browned face, not paying any mind to who was listening or whether her son heard her.

"I wear trunks in the hot springs 'cause I don't wanna be naked around my mom," said Keebler. It was the first thing he'd said. He had a downy caterpillar moustache and had tried to bleach his dark-blond hair lighter but merely succeeded in turning it orange. He only looked at me. Half-Peach sat silent as a rock.

"Oh please," screeched Pixie. "I'm your mumma, I've seen your pee-pee a million times. I changed your diapers, for crying out loud!"

This, like the rest of it, went ignored. "You like hip hop?" Keebler asked me and, I think, Half-Peach. "You like acid?" This got an enthusiastic affirmative from Half-Peach. "I got some paper that'll send you to outer space," Keebler grinned, showing long yellow teeth, like a rodent's. "You all are staying out at the slabs?"

Half-Peach said that we were.

"Great. I got the night off work. I'll come pick you up. We can drive around. I always trip balls in the desert."

Pixie stood up, displaying her tiny, childlike body. "What about me, Keebler?" she whined. "I don't got nothing going on tonight."

But Keebler was hoisting himself out of the pit and maybe he didn't hear her.

The car groaned and dragged over rocks, but Keebler didn't slow down.

He'd picked us up after nightfall, Half-Peach and me waiting for him out on the couch on Angel's slab. Keebler wore a track suit and had slicked back his hair. His car was a little sporty thing, low to the ground and painted a flashy royal blue. Special lights shone from the bottom of the car, from the roof, like a spaceship. Pixie waved from the passenger seat, her pupils wide as black buttons. Venom and Roxy leaned out of the back window, hooting and hollering.

"Hey!" said Half-Peach, already up and running toward the car.

Keebler said, "Found these guys walking on the road. They loved my wheels. Let's hit it."

We climbed into the back seat, Venom sitting on Roxy, and somehow I got squashed onto Half-Peach's lap, my neck curled to keep my head from bashing the ceiling. The car smelled like aftershave, cigarettes and weed. Pixie cranked up the car stereo. She was wearing a backward baseball cap. Hip hop roared from the dash, and she threw her hands around in time to the music.

Keebler climbed into the car and hit the gas. "Pass it back, moms," he said to Pixie as the car shot down the road. Pixie handed back a plastic baggie with little squares of paper inside. "Take your medicine, children," she crowed in her baby voice.

I looked over at Venom and Roxy. "I'm so fucked already," Venom said to no one.

The acid was bitter, and I chewed on it until it was soggy and shredded. The desert was opaque with blackness and the dashboard lights made the stars harder to see. The music was so loud it distorted, bass rumbling the seats and making my organs vibrate.

Keebler drove up from the flat plains of the desert into the hills and parked in front of an old bunker. We piled out chaotically. Pixie began doing jumping jacks. Roxy and Venom kissed sloppily. The new silence rang in my ears as I climbed from the car, the veins trembling in my body.

"This whole place used to be a military base," Keebler said, sitting on the hood of his car and lighting a joint. He hauled on it and passed it around. He'd left the lights from his car on. He was like a skinny alien, sitting there on the pile of metal and phosphorescence. "The desert is full of forgotten land mines. You could just be walking along and BLAM." He screamed the last word and it ricocheted through the darkness. Pixie giggled nervously, spinning in circles with her arms outstretched. "And there's all kinds of bunkers. Some of 'em are above ground like this one," and Keebler nodded at the hulking shell, a mass in the night, "but some of 'em are underground, buried by a thin layer of sand, and you won't know it's there until you fall in and break ya legs. Just a tomb under the ground."

Pixie said, "Turn on the music again, Keebler baby."

Venom pulled a pair of winter gloves from her back pocket. There were tiny lights on each fingertip, and she put the gloves on and made her hands into wings like a butterfly, leaving stripes of light against the blackness.

Keebler reached into the car and switched on the stereo, this time blasting a digital galactic techno beat. Pixie began dancing furiously, raising little clouds of dust.

"Come on," whispered Half-Peach, pulling me toward the bunker.

The noise fell away as we crept through the dry grass toward the concrete tube. The tin door had been peeled away from its frame, falling into the weeds. We ducked inside and were hit in the face by gasoline fumes.

"Don't light a cigarette," warned Half-Peach.

The ground was sandy and covered in garbage, old milk crates, cardboard, raggedy blankets. The walls of the bunker began to breathe, as if we were inside the belly of a whale.

From outside, Keebler shouted, "Let's go, let's go, come on!"

When we came back, everyone had piled into the car and Pixie was behind the wheel, squealing, "Fuji! Fuji! Fuji!"

"We're going to see my mom's friend Fuji," said Keebler, as I climbed onto Half-Peach's lap and slammed the door.

Pixie seemed to relish abusing Keebler's car. She slammed down on the gas, grinding with gusto over rocks and along rutted roads. The headlights lit up a small dirt path through the windshield but the entire world beyond was black. Keebler held the dashboard and hollered at his mother every time the vehicle jerked on the rough terrain.

I squeezed Half-Peach's hand as the car rocked, my head knocking into the roof. The dashboard lights swimming and circling, like we were in a tiny plane careening toward the water at a crazy rate. Venom and Roxy were pushed up against me, sweating and stinking and kissing with their mouths open. The stars seemed to be flying or falling into the weeds.

Pixie turned up the music, this time playing violent hip hop. Words like weapons pounded from the speakers, a man shouting about cutting people up, about dissecting his victims, about the abuse he suffered at the hands of his family, about the revenge he was going to take. Pixie knew all of the words and rapped along in her high-pitched voice, her baseball cap falling onto my feet.

We finally came to land on another hill, somewhere in the unmappable desert. There was a round aluminum trailer against the bush. The headlights picked out a man standing beside a campfire and holding a long staff. He had snow-white hair and a beard, wore a cargo vest with a scarf tied around his neck. He looked like an explorer. He raised his hand, open-palmed, to salute us as we climbed from the car.

"Hello Keebler, hello Pixie," he said. "I'm Fuji," he introduced himself to the rest of us.

"Fuji!" Pixie skipped over to the man and wrapped her arms around his waist, like a daughter hugging her father. He smiled benevolently at the top of her head.

We were on top of a great bluff. The land fell away just beyond the fire, to the infinite desert below, dark and unknowable.

Now that the car was silent and unlit, the stars came out in big bunches, heavy as white grapes. I stood on the edge of the cliff alone. I could hear Keebler telling Roxy, Venom and Half-Peach that Fuji was the father he'd never had, that Pixie met him out here at the slabs. Before this, Keebler said, he had been living in Hollywood, but he came back to Niland to care for his mother. He missed Hollywood every day. "What is here for me? What is here for me?" he said.

"You're a pussy," came Pixie's voice. It had suddenly lost its high-pitched syrup. "You're a fucking pussy, Keebler," she said. Her legs splayed out straight in front of her, her wrinkled face squeezed closed like a fist.

When I turned back to the fire, their faces orange and dancing, Pixie called to me, "You're a water pixie!"

Keebler was walking back to the car.

Half-Peach came up beside me in the dark. "Let's get a ride back to Angel's," they said. That was why I kept them close, especially in the dark. Because of the going-home-ness. We held hands and went to the car together, away from the cliff and the fire.

Venom and Roxy had a fight, that's what Angel said. Roxy went back to San Diego in the night, but Venom stayed behind. In the coming days, we saw her rarely. She slept on the skateboard slab with the boys and the dogs and the drugs. Sometimes I thought I could see her crazed silhouette twitching against the horizon, hear the ragged lash of her laughter in the twilight.

The late afternoon cooled down to a soft purple wash. Stoned, I watched my hand like a white watery weed as it reached out and grabbed for the carrots piled up on the table. I sliced vegetables into sections with a plastic-handled knife.

The evening was strangely subdued. Angel and Scooter had gone down to the springs for a soak. Even the skateboard slab was quiet. Half-Peach and I used each other's bodies to sit up straight. Sometimes I forgot we were two separate people. Travelling together had given us an indelible bond, our survival instincts as one. We had been in

Slab City for a month now, but it felt like we had always lived here. We touched each other to remind ourselves we both existed.

My relationship with Angel became strained because I wouldn't use my feminine wiles on the old men in town to get communal gas. Still, she loaned me a baking tray so I could bring Half-Peach breakfast in bed on their birthday. We stayed under our sleeping bags a long time, watching the sun move across the trailer ceiling, comforted by common acts of pleasure that came with us wherever we went.

After, we went out to the edge of the slabs where there had been a rumour of puppies. Down an old dirt path, away from most of the trailers, to a camp belonging to an old recluse. To be reclusive in Slab City meant you had fallen from the planet completely.

His was an isolated corner, messy with meaningless trash. Faded stuffed animals, board games, old rotary telephones, electrical wire tangled in the bushes like broken snakes.

"Hello?" My voice was swallowed up in the rippling waves of burnt sun. No one answered. The rusted trailer, boards in place of the wheels, creaked in the hot wind. Little Wing began sniffing under the structure, and three scrawny puppies came scrambling from the shadows to meet her, their fur matted and curly.

Half-Peach squatted in the dust, pups slinking around their ankles. They squinted up at me where I stood backlit against the sun, and I knew they hadn't yet found their dog.

A man came limping out from behind the trailer. "You all want somethin'?" Jetting after him came a mangy rat of a dog, her bark stabbing the air as she tried to get near her puppies who mingled with Little Wing. The man kicked his boot in her direction, and she shied away.

"We heard you had pups you were getting rid of," I answered, crossing my arms over my chest. I wondered how many puppies we could fit in our trailer. I tried not to blatantly glare at him. Flies with honey and all that. The man went over and grabbed the two white puppies still sniffing around, holding them by their scruffs.

"You want these vermin? Take 'em from me, then. The bitch won't stop getting herself knocked up, and now I got an infestation."

Half-Peach shoved their fists in their jean pockets. Like me, they were sensitive about small creatures. "Are there any boy puppies?"

The old man scowled, first at us, then at the mother dog, who had come slinking back, barking under her breath. He didn't want to do us any favours, but he also wanted to rid himself of the dogs. Finally, he shrugged one shoulder and said there was one boy pup, but he'd have to fish him out from beneath the trailer, which he went off and did.

After a few minutes of him scrambling in the dirt and wrestling off the mother dog, he extracted a squirming white pup in his grizzled hand.

This pup had sleek white fur, a long snout and short little legs. He had clear blue eyes and a pink nose with black freckles. Half-Peach found their birthday dog. They named him Two Star, because of the way his blue eyes shone.

Sound travelled for miles in the desert, and we heard the car coming before we saw it, tearing toward us along the dirt road, first a sparkle and then close enough to count the dents. The blue sedan looked like it had made a desperate escape from the suburbs and was now ravaged from turning up in the badlands. It ground to a stop beside Angel and Scooter's trailer, sending up a spray of yellow-brown gravel.

Alex leaped from the vehicle, his dreadlocks flying everywhere, wishing Half-Peach happy birthday and shouting about everything strange he'd seen lately, interrupting himself and trying to smoke a cigarette while he talked. He said he was ready for a nice, long, quiet stint in Slab City.

I couldn't stop looking at his car, its sleek blue hide glinting in the sun. All it took was four wheels and a little gas and you could find yourself out on a highway somewhere.

I elbowed Half-Peach in the ribs. They were looking at the car too. "Since it's my birthday," Half-Peach said slowly, "I'm stealing the car. All right, Alex? For my birthday, I'm gonna steal that car."

Alex was busy lighting a fire in the rusty fire pit, touching matches to the edges of sun-faded newspaper. Tongues of flame leaped up at the purple twilight, long fingers reaching for the coming stars. "Sure, Peach. You betcha."

In the distance, I could see Angel limping along toward us on the dirt path, Scooter holding her arm.

It was easy to wake up at dawn in Slab City. The light split the sky open and in five minutes went from inky blue to celestial sunshine, igniting the entire world. The locals were used to the sunrises and slept through them mostly, but Half-Peach and I still woke up excited. Maybe that was just our way.

I had a flap of cardboard and wrote on it, "Dear Alex, thank you for letting us steal your car. If you need it back head north. Enjoy Slab City. Angel and Scooter, thank you for everything."

Alex had fashioned himself a tent from a plastic sheet and slung it between two trees, far enough away that it would give us a head start. The trailers around us were silent, and the morning was fresh and cool in its newness.

The car had been parked on the edge of the Karma Kitchen slab. It was a Buick Skylark with three windows, the fourth being covered in cardboard and duct tape. There was a foot-sized dent in the back door. The trunk didn't open. Alex said he was given the car after he'd witnessed it crash into another vehicle in downtown San Diego. The man driving it saw Alex on the street and offered the vehicle to him. "It's not even worth the insurance," he'd said.

Cardboard signs littered the back seat. They said, *Better weather or spare change* and *In Love, Out of Gas*. Some of them had been ours and some of them must have been penned by other people along the way.

Half-Peach climbed into the front seat and turned the ignition. Alex had shown us how the car didn't need keys to start. I covered the dashboard with bouquets of dried roses and driftwood I'd kept in our little trailer. The car smelled of garbage and salt, the smell of the Pacific where it met the land.

We took out our road map and penned a route, writing *Fuck Venice* beside Los Angeles, because we vowed never to be stuck there again. And then we pulled away from the Karma Kitchen slab, down the dusty road, past the dried bones of the trees, Salvation Mountain like a melted wedding cake in the sun, and over the wide white road of the desert, away from Slab City.

Sur

"Mind if we pull over?" Half-Peach asked me.

"I wanna get to the Henry Miller Library before dark," I protested. But I didn't want to rush, either, through the cool green chill of the hilly winding roads, the damp, dark quiet. We were fresh from Slab City with the Buick Skylark, and our road freedom gave me beatnik excitement.

Half-Peach pulled to the side of the highway anyway, just so we could keep looking out at the open mouth of the sea, the wide line of space, the blue beneath us. The tree trunks, thick as houses, crowded against the road. A ladybug skittered across my sunburn. The edge of the cliff falling away so far below made my knees sing.

We'd been driving since the desert. We'd found a pack of Marlboros in a puddle, jaundiced and damp. They had the flavour of fermented pennies, but we smoked them anyway because we had nothing else.

The air up here was thin and clear. It was just the two of us, Half-Peach and me. The dogs, Little Wing with her black fur and Half-Peach's birthday puppy, Two Star, with his white fur, sat expectantly in the back seat as if they were headed to a wedding.

"Jack Kerouac and Henry Miller," I kept saying, like a child at Christmas reciting the gifts she wants.

The sky glittered a cold, clean diamond blue. Half-Peach parked the Skylark on the unpaved driveway, and we walked toward the low porch.

There were three others sitting there. We recognized them by the way they dressed, by the way they wore their hair. They were like us. An old black dog and a van parked nearby, an acoustic guitar and a road map they'd drawn themselves. The girl's name was Mandy, and the boys were David and Kurt, both of them dreadlocked and over-alled. Mandy was from Manitoba—it was reassuring to know my country hadn't been erased behind me.

She told us she'd picked the boys up on a highway in North Dakota. "We're headed down to Los Angeles. We could form a caravan," she offered. But I told her we weren't going back that way again.

We went into the library that looked more like a chapel, its books hanging from the high ceiling like hovering doves. The silence didn't come from the building, nor from the deep crush of trees, but from the poems framed on the walls.

"You missed Neil Young last night. We hid in the bushes and watched," Mandy said. "There's a campground down the road we've been sneaking into for showers. You wanna carpool?"

I knew the scarce luxury of a hot shower now. My body felt like it had built its own natural coating against the harsher elements of the world. My hair had formed mats at the back. Half-Peach had a ring of perpetual grime around their neck. There was nothing sanitary about living on the road.

Half-Peach got into the back of the van with the boys and giddily accepted the bottle of rum Kurt offered. "People say they love travelling with me," they had reminded me on the highway. Because somewhere back there, it began to feel as if we were inmates sharing an ankle chain, and I didn't know why.

Mandy drove us over the curving road that ran into the woods and then out along the rocky sides of the hills clinging with trees, white V-shaped birds dipping and disappearing in the mists. Rain knocked on the windshield and went away again, like a neighbour calling on an empty house.

The campground was closed, but there was no gate across the driveway winding into the cave of trees. Mandy barrelled over the gravel. She told me she'd been hanging around Big Sur for a week with David and Kurt, sleeping on cliffs overlooking the ocean and planning their adventure south.

Mandy was a confident driver, sitting ramrod straight, her thick honey-coloured hair tucked behind her ears. She parked half in the bush so no one would discover the van and led the way through the shadowy grounds to a shower hut. The floors were cement, fluorescent light tubes over a set of mirrors. I saw my grimy reflection in the glass and couldn't believe it belonged to me. The matted brown hair, the skinny face, the bad skin. I reminded myself the body was nothing but a case to cart my spirit around in. The sentiment was meant to make me feel better.

"Want some?" Mandy held out a backpack full of hotel soaps and sample shampoos. "It's great having a girl around," she said, pumping the paper towel dispenser vigorously so we'd have something to dry off with. "Carting lost boys has its place, but being a female explorer is different than being a male explorer. We always have more to lose."

"Amen to that," I said, shedding my crusty clothes and stepping into the plastic shower stall. I made the water as hot as I could stand, my skin blooming pink flowers in the steam.

I was used to washing at public bathroom sinks, industrial soap and rough brown paper towel, someone knocking on the door to hurry me up. I stood in the stall trying to store up as much of the hot water as I could for the days when I would be without the privilege.

If I was in Big Sur with money. If I could go to the woods and find a quiet cabin. If I didn't bombard the landscape with my stupid poverty and childish anarchy. If I was alone. If I could drive. If I wasn't. If I hadn't.

When I pulled the shower curtain open, Mandy was already gone.

I stood in front of the mirror and brushed my teeth with my sandy toothbrush, ran my fingers through my wet hair. The only sound was the wind rattling the tree branches. I pulled on clothes I'd washed in the ocean, warm from the car and smelling of salt.

There was a crunch of footsteps outside and I expected Mandy to poke her head in and tell me to hurry up, but the door came in violently, banging against the wall. A man scowled from the door frame. "Coming in here is forbidden. I should call the police." He crossed his hairy forearms over his chest, a walkie-talkie crackling from behind him.

A hatred flared up in me. I hated men like him, just as he must have hated grubby little hippies like me. I pushed past with exaggerated haughtiness. "Call them. I got what I needed."

"Where were you?" Half-Peach demanded when I climbed into the van. The smell of rum came off them in waves. I didn't answer.

Mandy drove along the dirt roads flanked by hanging trees. When the sun finally pushed its way out of the mist, she pulled over so we could walk along the edge of the woods. A stream ran beside us, houses peeking from the foliage. A lone ribbon of birdsong striking the sky.

Other than Half-Peach, Kurt and David passing around the emptying bottle of rum, we didn't say much. Big Sur had a way of mellowing out our strangled city nerves.

We strolled along the empty dirt road, Mandy and me walking side by side, the others up ahead. I wondered how easy it used to be, to come up here and take a cottage in the forest, to write and live on tins of beans.

We came across a little yellow house, empty for the season and tucked back against the bush. Its windows were dark, and the front garden was wild with brambles. We sat on the front stoop and I pretended, like I always pretended, that this place was mine.

Half-Peach had the guitar with them and played Bob Dylan. They turned around to puke discreetly in the flower bed.

That night, Mandy, Kurt and David showed us where they'd been parking to sleep. We followed their van in the Skylark, pulling onto a grassy bank overlooking the sea. Stars reflected down onto the water in rippling pinpricks. Half-Peach wanted to make a fire, but Mandy warned them the local police roamed the hills looking for punks like us. We said goodnight.

Half-Peach and I unrolled our sleeping bags in the back seat and climbed in with the dogs. Sleeping in a car was almost like sleeping in a house. The seat was comfy, like a bed. I felt okay. I could sleep. And in the morning, we could drive away. Set up our little house in a whole new place, begin again.

The damp of Big Sur crawled into my joints until I hobbled like an old man. It was the hip pain that woke me in the morning, gloom pushing against the car windows. I untangled myself from the pile of sleeping bags in the back seat. The dogs ran in the wet grass, peeing on the tires.

Fog sneaked through the giant pines, trundling silently down the road in great opaque banks. Rain came and went, came and went. I stood on the cliff edge, wet, cold grass beneath my toes, and stared out into the greyness. The sea was down there somewhere, I could smell its deep, dank body. The early cry of gulls. The wind across the water.

Mandy climbed out of the van. "If there was ever a day to leave for Southern California, it'd be today," she said.

I wanted to jump in the van with her and go, just the two of us. I wanted to be with women in the sun. I missed

Kriel. I thought of Jay. But Mandy went to wake up Kurt. "We kissed last night," she said, breathless.

Half-Peach came out of the Skylark to scowl at the weather. "I want breakfast. You wanna come?" they asked Mandy and the boys, who were blinking sleepily from the van.

"I think we're going to hit the road," said Mandy. She turned to see if the boys agreed.

We said goodbye in the dark greens and blacks and greys, watched the van pull away from the edge of the cliff and down into the trees, headed south. I stood there until my arms were beaded with moisture. I could only see the empty road, Half-Peach already waiting for me behind the wheel.

When we started driving, I remembered the dream.

I'd been walking along an empty beach. The sky was monarch butterfly orange. I'd come to a wooden dock jutting out into a blank stretch of water. I went out onto the planks, wobbling, and when I looked around, I was completely surrounded by the water, black and infinite.

From beneath came movement, a ripple becoming a hulking plateau buoying up from beneath the surface. A glistening gorgon of barnacles and twitching blue-black muscle and one sparkling yellow eye, sad whorls forming the socket. A humpback whale.

It lifted up its streaming tail as if to smite me, the tensing fist of my heart. But instead, the tail lowered until it cupped my entire body like a cold, wet hand. I stood still on the bobbing shingle, smelling the dank seaweed smell, and was back on the sand.

Then I saw a girl walking along the edge of the water. She had dark green skin and orange hair the same colour as the sky. And I thought she looked just like me.

Golden City

Instead of heading north to San Francisco, Half-Peach decided to drive to Santa Barbara to visit friends first. "That's the luxury of the car," they argued. "We can drive all over the place!"

I loved driving up and down the One, along the coast, nothing but the ocean beside us. I started not wanting to get out of the car at all. I was warm and lazy, packed in with the dogs. We drove and drove, consulting maps like holy books. The car was a capsule, cozy and safe, like a tiny ship at sea.

We blew a tire on the highway outside Santa Barbara.

The ominous sound of flapping rubber filled the car and Half-Peach pulled over to examine the damage. The tire was completely shredded.

"Fuck," they said, leaning against the blue hood and pushing their straw hat back on their forehead.

I stepped out of the car to wait with them. It was eerie, the stillness—not having a motor beneath us moving us forward. The highway was hot in the morning, the air golden and welcome after the grey-green damp of Big Sur.

We hadn't been waiting long before some good Samaritan, a cheerful suburban hippie, pulled over and changed the wasted rim to a donut tire. "It's a good omen," Half-Peach told me, as we drove the peg-legged car off the highway. "We're supposed to go to Santa Barbara."

But sitting in the car had chafed my shoulder raw and the skin burned. I sat forward to keep it from touching. I'd woken up sick in the early morning. I wanted to drive straight on to San Francisco. The detour made me nervous.

We drove up to the house on the hill like tin cans blown by the wind, wheezing and exhausted. When Half-Peach shut off the motor, it was if the Buick's heart had finally stopped.

There was a man in the driveway, leaning over his motorcycle. He straightened up as our car pulled in, putting a wrench in his back pocket. His handshake was oily. "Franky told me you were coming and that you'd need some repairs." He nodded at the Buick. "Quite a vehicle you got there," he said. He smiled under his moustache as he saw the dented door, the patched up window. Half-Peach showed him how we started the ignition without keys, and he got a kick out of it.

"Half-*Peach*!" A girl came running from the house with bracelets jangling, her wispy boyfriend coming along behind. Each of them had a handshake like a limp rag. "You *made* it." They were friends from Illinois. Franky had the face of a praying mantis, bulging eyes and pincer-like teeth crowded into a tiny mouth. Her boyfriend wore a dress, his hair bleached white.

Franky led us inside, up a pile of stairs to the bedroom at the top of the rambling house. The room's one window looked out on the road, no other houses in sight. There was something lonely about the house, a feeling of passing through someone else's dream.

A ferret cage took up the corner of the room, and the whole place reeked of sawdust and stink glands. Instead of a window curtain, they had an American flag. And bunk beds. Franky held a match to a bundle of raggedy sage and blew the pale leaves until its dank smoke almost covered the ferret stench.

"You can stay however long you want," said Franky. "I talked to Linda, it's her house. We've been here for two years, but people are always coming through. Moe works at the movies, so we can see them for free." She indicated her blond boyfriend, sprawled on the bottom bunk.

Moe said, "My job is shit."

Someone knocked on the door, and Franky jingled along to investigate, ushering in a woman in her mid-forties. She looked like a Neil Young song with her leather jacket and red lipstick. "Welcome to the house," she said, her voice strong and gravelly. "You met Dean downstairs and I'm Linda. If you need anything while you're getting your tire fixed, don't think twice. I'm nursing at the hospital mostly, but I'm reachable." To Franky, she said, "Me and Dean are going to dinner. We'll be back late, we're taking the hog." Waggling her eyebrows girlishly, she backed out into the hallway, calling over her shoulder, "And take care of those weasels. Your room smells like an asshole."

"Thinks she's my mother," Franky sulked. "Let's go up to the attic. Dorvan owes me weed." She went out into the hallway and shouted at a square hole in the ceiling. "Dorvan! Let us in."

A rope ladder trickled down to the carpet. Franky tugged it to make sure it was secure and then pulled herself up. Half-Peach followed behind her, nose up her skirt.

Dorvan sat cross-legged on his sheetless mattress, a dictionary on his lap piled high with marijuana. The attic had no windows, and the walls had been painted blood red. Half of Dorvan's head was shaved down to the pale scalp, but the other half, perfectly divided, hung long and stringy to his shoulder. He sat shirtless, defiantly thin, beneath a light bulb hanging from the slanted roof.

As soon as we were settled on the floor, Dorvan reached over and turned on the stereo. The plastic machine began to tremble under a barrage of Black Sabbath. We smoked, unable to speak over the screaming music, and then made our way dizzily back down the rope ladder. My feet had barely touched the floor when Dorvan yanked the ladder up, sliding a piece of raw wood over the hole.

"I gotta go to work," Moe said, looking like he'd just received a piece of tragic news.

"That's fine, we'll all go to the movies," said Franky. And then reminded him, "You have to sneak us in. I'll drive."

Half-Peach and I sat in the back seat of Franky's Volvo. My shoulder burned and I sat forward, hot and nauseous.

Moe and Franky gossiped about a hippie around town we didn't know while I watched State Street stream past the window, decorated with tiny white fairy lights. The red terracotta roofs and sandy buildings, arched pillared doorways and leaning palms, made the whole town look like a party, sugar, icing, promise.

When we got to the theatre, Moe split off from us despondently and Half-Peach, Franky and I slipped into the cool theatre. When I closed my eyes and let the colours wash over me, incubated in the popcorn-scented darkness, I could have been anywhere.

When I woke up the next morning, my skin burned like battery acid on the right side of my body. In the bathroom I tried to pull off my T-shirt but it had stuck to the skin with hardened runoff. When the fabric came up, it revealed a shredded swath of leaking sores. In the mirror, I saw the entire side of my face was covered in blisters, spreading up the side of my cheek toward my eye.

Half-Peach was lying on the bedroom floor with

Franky, and they were whispering amongst themselves when I came in.

"You got some some kinda rash." Half-Peach glanced over. "It's everywhere. What happened? Poison ivy?"

"Better go show Linda," Franky told me.

Linda and I stood in the kitchen and she put on a pair of rubber gloves, rubbing aloe vera over the tattered sores. "You don't have any way of seeing a doctor, do you?"

"No ..." I said. "I'm Canadian."

"You can't leave something like this. See how it's around your eye like that? This is shingles, honey. You can go to the homeless shelter on Tuesday if you can wait that long. They got a doctor there."

It was Friday. "I can wait," I said. I would wait and it would go away. "Maybe the tire will be fixed by then." And we could keep moving on.

Franky and Half-Peach wanted to get ice cream. They wanted to play music on the street corner, Half-Peach with their banjo and Franky with her tambourine. When I went to a café to use the toilet, I saw myself in the mirror again, blistered, infected.

"Don't feel like you have to hang out with us if you don't want to," Half-Peach said when I came back out. They strummed on the banjo, laughing with a tourist who stopped to talk.

"You can walk back to the house if you're bored," Franky added.

I sat back down on the wall. "I'm fine," I said.

By Tuesday morning, Dean had replaced the tire on the Buick Skylark. Franky got a new job and Moe was working doubles all week. It was time to move on.

"Guess I gotta take you to the doctor before we head for 'Frisco," Half-Peach said as we climbed into the car.

"Guess so." I sat with my elbows on my knees so my back wouldn't rub on the seat. My body was slowing down on me. It was like trying to run underwater.

The homeless shelter resembled an old barn, cement floors and plywood walls. The doctor's office had been built out of drywall. When I sat down on a plastic chair, a volunteer came over and told me I couldn't see the doctor until four o'clock that afternoon. Half-Peach sighed at the wall clock and went out to sleep in the car.

"I think I have shingles," I told the doctor when I finally saw him. He was a weary man in a white coat. I sat on the crinkling paper sheet and lifted up my shirt.

"Hold on, hold on, fill these out first," he said and pushed a pile of documents at me. "You're too young to get shingles. It's probably scabies. Do you have anxiety? Sometimes people get a rash from anxiety."

"I'm not anxious," I promised him and left the forms beside me to show him my skin, the burst blisters along my ribs and along my neck, the bumps all over the side of my face, the sores on my eyelid.

The doctor cleared his throat, his hand hovering and then retreating. "Ah. Yes." He pulled out a ballpoint pen and scribbled a note. "Yes, all right. That is shingles." He gestured toward my backpack on the floor, then gestured at my body. "A person your age would get shingles from immune system compromise. Poor diet. Exposure to germs. You could have lost the eye. Lost your hearing. If this spread to the organs, you would have an inflamed liver. Spine. Brain. You people know you have access to a free doctor here in town. You shouldn't have waited so long."

"I'm not American."

"Ah."

"And I don't have any money for medicine. If this isn't some fatal thing, I'll be on my way."

The doctor rolled his eyes. "All right, all right, no need to be melodramatic. Let me make a phone call." He punched in a number on the desk phone, pinched the bridge of his nose, came back to life when someone answered. "Varicella zoster virus. Gone to the eye. No insurance. No, it's at the outreach clinic." When he hung up the phone, he reached for his pen and began fiddling with it irritably. I was going to be a lot of paperwork. "Do you have transportation? Can you take the bus, perhaps?"

"I got a car."

"Okay. I'm going to give you the address to a hospital. They're going to provide you with medication. You're
going to take *this coupon*"—he scrawled furiously onto a
piece of paper— "and you have to bring it to *this address*,
but you have to be there within the next thirty minutes or
we can't help you. These pills are not narcotics. They're for
your immune system. Understand?"

"I understand." I hopped off the table and went to
wake up Half-Peach.

Driving down the One with fog across the rocks, the city
of San Francisco opening up like a mouth full of electric
teeth.

I was completely out of it. The drugs were doing weird
things to my vision. My hair fell out, my joints hurt, I kept
falling asleep.

Half-Peach was taking us to their aunt's house in
Chinatown. We didn't speak for the entire drive. I slept a
drugged sleep, my face pressed against the window.

The houses were like melting cakes in the rain, paint
bright as sugar, hills tossing and turning in the mist. Half-
Peach ran a red light and a truck almost bulldozed my side
of the car.

"You could have fucking killed me," I yelled as the driver leaned on its horn, shaking his fist at us.

"Well, you're still alive," Half-Peach, who never raised their voice, yelled back.

We pulled into a parking lot somewhere behind the reds and golds of Chinatown. The night had come down, twinkling in raindrops and street lights on our windshield. A little brown car pulled in beside us and two Filipino women got out, the aunt tall and thin, the grandmother small and leaning on a walker. They came over and rapped their knuckles on Half-Peach's window.

"We're back here." The tall one indicated a building across the parking lot. They ignored me.

Their apartment smelled like a Catholic hospital, stale bibles and blankets, linoleum and must. I followed Half-Peach and the relatives inside

Their tiny unit was on the fifth floor. When we walked inside, Half-Peach and I silenced the formerly raucous room. Only the television in the corner continued to noisily blast a Filipino soap opera.

It was ten at night, and a little baby girl came running up to Half-Peach with a bottle full of cola. Half-Peach tugged her pigtail and she shied away.

The rest of them stared at us. At me. And then they all began speaking in Filipino. Half-Peach sat down at the table. I leaned against the kitchen counter.

There was white rice, Coca-Cola, a soup with clear noodles, a bowl of gristly chicken. The baby sat in front of the television, her diaper squashing against the floor.

"Lee, your skin has gotten so dark," the grandmother admonished, stroking their cheek with her knuckly finger.

"I dunno, Grandma. I've been in the sun." They shrugged, poured a glass of Coke. "You want some?" I shook my head.

"When are you going to marry a nice Filipino girl?" the aunt demanded. She spooned rice onto a plate and handed it to me without looking, then sat beside Half-Peach, rubbing her hand through their black hair.

The relatives asked about other family members, reminding Half-Peach to call their mother and father.

I sat on the sofa in the living room. The little girl curled up against my leg, and we watched the soap together, neither of us able to make sense of the story.

The wall was covered in crucifixes. There was a sepia photograph of Half-Peach's grandmother when she was a young woman, her face sharp and beautiful. Beside the photo was a ceramic statue of Mary, her eyes forlorn beneath her blue mantle. Half-Peach finally sat beside me. We'd had to leave the dogs down in the car, and I worried about them.

"Lee," the aunt called from the kitchen, "we're going to bed. You want to sleep in your cousin's room?"

"We'll probably sleep on the living room floor, Aunty. It's fine."

The grandmother rose up terribly from the table. "You're going to sleep *together*?" And she finally looked at me, her narrow face full of wrath. This was too much for her. She shuffled off to her bedroom, making a noise that sounded like "Bah!" and shut the door behind her.

"I'm sorry," Half-Peach whispered from the floor.

I lay on the couch and pretended to sleep. The street light slashed through the living room. They began to snore, and I needed to pee. But the bathroom was in the grandmother's bedroom.

I crept out of the apartment and into the hallway, the walls flickering under the lights, out onto the balcony. The sliding doors closed behind me. I pissed onto the creeping plants. When I went back to the doors and pulled, I realized they had locked behind me.

The dark, wet San Francisco night wrapped around the balcony, stars frigidly dripping. I sat down on the cold concrete. What would happen in the morning? I don't know how long I was out there for. I shivered and pulled my knees to my chest. When I closed my eyes, the doors slid open. Half-Peach stood there backlit, a sleepy apparition.

"Come on," they said. "Come back inside." And they pulled me up with their hands.

We left early in the morning. I thanked the aunt and grandmother for their hospitality. They thanked me for leaving.

Half-Peach and I went to the San Francisco Public Library, the main branch. It was a modern building that looked more like an airport. The interior still had that old smell of paper pages and book spines, the organic aroma of words, like all the others. But I knew this library was different. It was a library on the edge of a precipice.

I wandered through the stacks. Old homeless men slept on chairs. Students frantically thumbed through volumes. Librarians pushed their book carts past me. The familiar markers of this sanctuary, this institution, rolled around me. This ersatz library. This Judas library. This final library.

In the main branch of the San Francisco Public Library, I picked up the pay phone receiver and called my parents. "Hi, don't hang up," I said. There was a long silence. They didn't say anything, but they were breathing, listening. "I just need somewhere to sleep for a week or two," I told them. We were a precarious family, a family built on contracts and negotiations, long distances and misunderstandings. I was glad to have a floor I couldn't fall below, but maybe I would have been better off without it. So many people didn't have parents. The old men sleeping in library chairs didn't have parents. I was not a prodigal son. I had gone out into the world and wrecked myself, but there would be no homecoming, no forgiveness. I just needed a place to sleep for a few weeks, and then I'd be gone again.

They laid out the conditions for my return and I agreed and hung up the phone. Then I went out to the car where Half-Peach was waiting for me. They drove me to the airport.

Veins of highways, grand canyons of skin. Mountain passes on the backs of hands, freeways on the insides of wrists, the biggest, thickest, bluest veins. As if someone knew how much we would need those hands to hitch a ride, to hold on tight.

I wasn't allowed to bring Little Wing with me. The airport security said I needed vaccination papers, registration. It was just as well. If I was going to leave California with my bag of pills, I might as well leave my little dog behind with Half-Peach and the rest of it. What would she do indoors, anyway? She had only known the free world. I handed her over to Half-Peach. I looked down into her liquid eyes, her brows knit together in concern. We'd been friends for so long. I'd forgotten life before her, the shades of loneliness. I was so used to carrying her little body around in my arms, holding her small warmth to me at night, worrying over her needs. When I handed Little Wing over at last, her absence was immediate, the emptiness was absolute.

Beyond the glass of the airport doors, the sun was setting. As I walked through the gate, I could hear Half-Peach call to nobody, "Where's my two-star system?" Because we had been a binary star in the cosmos. Because we were a two-body problem. Because who could predict our trajectory now.

Ouroboros

"I don't think you should come back to California anytime soon," Half-Peach told me. The phone roared with static to remind us how far apart we were. It was our first phone call since I'd left, two weeks ago. Years ago. They said they'd met up with old friends from Northern California and were headed east on foot. They wouldn't be near a phone again for who knew how long. They said the police were looking for us. "We're on wanted posters all over the place."

"I didn't know they still did those."

"They do in America. They want us for questioning. We're the last ones who saw her alive, apparently."

I went over to the bedroom window and sucked in lungfuls of cold Canadian air. The apartment was so quiet. I had almost made enough money to leave again. I didn't think about where I was. I wasn't really there.

"Who are you talking about?"

"That girl called Venom. They found her five miles from Slab City with her hands cut off. They found girls in ditches in the desert. I don't know how many others.

All of them with no hands. The cops want to know what happened."

"But I don't know," I said. "I don't know what happened."

Acknowledgements

I would like to thank mentors such as Josip Novakovich and Mikhail Iossel. Thank you to my agent, Barbara Berson, for her incredible support of this book and my work, and to my editors, Caroline Skelton and Nicola Goshulak, for helping me to make sense of this story.

Thank you to Kriel, Keyzon, Alex, Izzy, Michael, Angel and Scooter, Puck and Brian, and Chief, and all of the other people with whom I found friendship along the way.

And thank you to my family.

This book is dedicated to the memory of James.